Growing Marijuana

for Beginners

A Step-by-Step Guide on Growing Medical Weed for Personal Use at Home. Indoor and Outdoor Cannabis Growing Techniques

© Copyright by **Jerry H. Rucker**

Table of Contents

INTRODUCTION

This is the tutorial for you if you want to start cultivating marijuana but are overwhelmed by a thousand uncertainties and queries. It's important to understand that it's not about having any exceptional abilities.

To begin this adventure, you must first learn the fundamentals of the marijuana plant, which will enable you to optimize your labor and achieve the greatest results, as well as the wonderful satisfaction that comes with becoming an expert in growing this plant. Marijuana cultivation needs a great deal of care, attention, and specific knowledge, as well as a great deal of dedication, perseverance, and even money.

If you follow this guide, you will also find that it is possible to achieve great results in any climate, although it may seem complicated and you can choose to try growing it indoors or outdoors.

Indoor marijuana growing allows you to produce marijuana at any time of year, regardless of the weather. Indoor marijuana cultivation has not only made cannabis cultivation more accessible to everyone, but it has also made it possible for the typical marijuana consumer to avoid feeding organized criminals. You will no longer require the services of drug traffickers if you grow your own marijuana. Your main objective is self-sufficiency, which you can easily achieve if you put your mind to it.

It is, of course, the grower's obligation to develop and maintain the environment in which the plants will thrive while growing indoors with artificial lights. It will always be him, not Mother Nature, who will have to look after the cannabis and regulate all of the growth criteria. If you want to grow your own marijuana inside and enjoy it, you'll need to be willing to monitor your female marijuana plants for at least three months.

Cannabis cultivation is a very specialised operation that necessitates specialized equipment. The initial costs include lighting kits, fans, and activated carbon filters, as well as pots, fertilizers, substrates, and Grow Box cabinets. Each cannabis crop necessitates a one-time investment as well as ongoing expenses such as power. However, after one or two harvests, you'll see that the costs are significantly lower than what you'd pay a drug dealer for the same amount.

Remember that marijuana cultivation does not end with harvest; appropriate drying and storage are critical for preventing mould and preserving the scent and freshness of the finished product.

All of this and more can be found in this necessary, straightforward, and complete handbook, which is also appropriate for newcomers to the world of marijuana.

American Legislation

The debate on its use has always been very heated. It must be said that the medical use of the substance is now legalized in many parts of the world: marijuana is, in fact, useful in the treatment of certain diseases, especially those that degenerate the nervous system. Marijuana legislation changes from country to country and in the United States it changes from region to region. These are which states in the United States are allowed to consume, sell and deliver cannabis.

If you imagine a map of the USA, you can consider four categories of states that have responded differently to the legalization of cannabis:

1. Some states have legalized marijuana.

2. Others have allowed its use for medical purposes only.

3. Some have decriminalized it.

4. In the minority, we find states where marijuana is still illegal.

As many as 14 states belong to the first category

At first it was only nine:

- ✓ Colorado
- ✓ Maine
- ✓ Vermont
- ✓ Oregon
- ✓ Washington
- ✓ Nevada
- ✓ Alaska
- ✓ the district of Columbia with the capital Washington
- ✓ Massachusetts

These were joined in 2018 by California and recently by the State of New York, New Jersey and New Mexico.

As a marijuana user, whether you are an American citizen or a tourist, you can not only use marijuana personally for recreational and medical purposes, but also buy it and produce it.

But what are the rules you have to follow to buy cannabis.

All the United States that have legalized cannabis have placed a number of restrictions on the sale and use of cannabis products.

Firstly, you must be of legal age, i.e. 21 years of age.

Places used for the sale of the products must be authorized by the authorities of the individual states and must be located at least 180 meters away from schools and hospitals. In addition, inside the shops, you can buy the product but not consume it.

The quantity was also limited. For example, in Nevada, Alaska, California and Colorado, the maximum daily purchase is one ounce, equivalent to 21 grams.

In Oregon and Washington, on the other hand, you can buy up to 1.16 ounces per day if the hemp product is in solid form, and 72 ounces if it is in liquid form. Finally, in the capital, the maximum daily quantity is 2 ounces.

In most states, the rules for the sale and consumption of tobacco are very similar to those of tobacco.

In fact, you cannot smoke in public places or near hospitals and schools. Instead, you can consume at home or in places not open to the public.

But that's not all: in all countries it is strictly forbidden to drive while smoking marijuana or after consuming it.

If more than 5 nanograms of active THC are detected per 1 ml of blood, you are subject to a penalty.

Personal cultivation of cannabis plants is also allowed in some states.

For example, in Alaska, up to 6 plants can be grown, while in California the limit is 3. In Oregon, up to 4 plants can be grown.

Finally, there are also guidelines for the possible export of the product outside of the individual state. The most restrictive one is Oregon, where you can buy and sell, but not take it outside the borders.

The 17 states where marijuana is totally illegal are;

- ✓ Alabama
- ✓ Georgia
- ✓ Idaho
- ✓ Indiana
- ✓ Iowa
- ✓ Kansas
- ✓ Kentucky
- ✓ Mississippi
- ✓ Nebraska
- ✓ North Carolina
- ✓ South Carolina
- ✓ South Dakota
- ✓ Tennessee
- ✓ Texas
- ✓ Virginia
- ✓ Wisconsin
- ✓ Wyoming

CHAPTER 1 – Grow Room Setup

Like any other plant, cannabis needs the right conditions to be able to flower or reproduce, so we will have to make sure to give it a more or less rich soil, a change of air, a good recirculation inside the growing room and to finish off with a light suitable for the surface to be illuminated.

None of these components should be overlooked, everything must be designed harmoniously: the lighting system must be supported by an air treatment sized according to the correct management of environmental parameters.

To help us in the control of these environmental parameters, temperature and relative humidity, it is advisable to outline a cultivation space, a growbox is the most practical solution. Not everyone is skilled in DIY and the offer of specialized shops is really varied and for all pockets, materials and finishes are to be considered fundamental in the choice of a grow box, a thick fabric and a good diamond mylar are superior to thin, transparent and non-reflective sheets, better to spend a few tens of euros more and not be afraid of any infiltration that during the cycle could cause stress to the plants.

Growbox

Growboxes can be divided into two categories:

> ➤ Up to 1 sqm: this category includes all the small and medium growboxes, those easily concealable and very practical. Perfect for beginners because they have a reduced volume and a surface area that allows you to use lamps easily manageable even by the most novice grower without affecting the environmental parameters.

> ➤ Over 1 sqm: all medium-large growboxes, for those who need a lot of space and already have some experience, require the use of one or more lamps that produce a lot of heat, proportionally sized vacuum cleaners and a large number of pots.

Once we have found the space to position our new grow box, we need to start looking around to find the best solution to combine spending, yield and discretion.

In recent years I've often found myself advising what to buy and I've had sudden changes in setups, small spaces where you can readjust things accumulated over time and new things to be placed side by side, in fact always try to shop in perspective, growing indoor is not cheap and often a better purchase today can save you money tomorrow.

As a result of the choice of the grow box we will have to think about how to illuminate our cultivation.

We know that we will hardly get more than the famous g/w, the ratio between yield in grams and watts consumed, so choosing the lamp according to this parameter can mean that the amount of harvest can be predicted at the beginning of the cycle.

For the moment we are not interested in the type of lighting, we will go into that later, for now we will limit ourselves to the amount of watts enough to well illuminate the surface of our box, in fact, the major companies that sell growboxes have standard sizes that we can find in various catalogues and are sizes such as 60x60x150, 120x60x180, 120x240x240 and so on up to sizes that are close to 20 square meters.

Below we will analyse three different types, those that are the largest among the new growers, from a small 60×60 to the more comfortable and spacious 100×100.

img360x60x150

This is an entry level model, it is discreet because of its small size, easily camouflaged and does not affect the household economy, it can be illuminated with any type of lighting with low wattages, does not require very powerful vacuum cleaners and produces little noise. In short, a perfect roommate.

Recommended lamps: up to 250w.

80x80x160

It differs little from its smaller brother, but more practical in terms of space, a larger volume allows you to dare a little more in terms of lighting. If combined with the right vacuum cleaner you can also use higher wattages.

Recommended lamps: up to 400w.

100x100x180

Unlike the two previous formats the growing area and volume increase and allow us to evaluate the use of powerful light sources such as 600w HPS, if temperatures allow, and we expect heavy harvests.

Recommended lamps: up to 600w.

CHAPTER 2 – Outdoor self-production: where to start

Weather and climate

In order to overcome unpleasant surprises of all kinds, the climate must be fully exploited. We advise you to choose varieties of seeds suitable for your latitudes. Another important aspect to take into account is the average temperature, even at night, of the area you choose for self-production, as well as exposure to wind and of course light.

Choose your seed

Within the vast panorama of seedbanks, there are generally at least three categories of seeds: regular, feminized and auto flowering. In the last years, thanks to the progress made in the scientific field on the use of CBD in medicine, a new category within the catalogues has taken over: the varieties with a high CBD content. This new type of plants can be feminized or auto flowering, in both cases the innovation lies in the THC/CBD ratio which is usually 1:1 (e.g. 10% THC/10% CBD).

To germinate your cannabis seeds in the right way, you first need to decide which seeds to grow and where to buy them, looking for reliable seedbanks with a history of success. If possible, get advice from your trusted grow shop. Beginners may want to start with an Indica-dominant variety that will remain small and squat with a short flowering period; otherwise Sativa-dominant varieties tend to stretch more and have longer flowering times.

It is often the case that a seed company claims their product ripens in 60 days, but this is hardly ever a definite harvest date. Some companies lower flowering times in an attempt to convince you to buy their seeds, a simple but effective marketing strategy.

You also need to take into account the downtime that plants take to recover from stress caused by transplanting or other aggravating factors; sometimes this can add weeks to the flowering phase and significantly push harvest time forward.

Germination, the beginning of a new life

Starting to germinate a seed is like giving birth to a new life, one of the most common mistakes that newbies make is to treat seeds as inanimate objects. You have to be gentle and ensure optimal conditions for proper germination. Below we will illustrate two basic techniques to ensure the success of our investment.

Wet germination. Some people choose to use a method that involves placing the seed in a damp paper or cotton cloth: this method consists of placing the seeds on a plate between two dampened strips of paper, covered by a second plate. Within a couple of days, you should see the seed open and a bud emerge. Immediately and carefully (using tweezers), the seed should be placed in the substrate and watered gently. There is nothing inherently wrong with using this method, as long as you operate carefully and do not let the sprout grow too long before planting it.

Germination in substrate. If you have decided to seed in substrate the process is even easier, you need to apply a hole in the middle of the pre-moistened substrate. Drop the seed about a quarter of an inch deep, cover the seed with a little soil and pat it gently.

Soil selection

Selecting a good growing medium is the first step towards a good harvest. Be careful that any type of domestic cultivation, whether indoor or outdoor, starts with the choice of seed and growing method. Buying cheap potting soil or choosing to use the soil in your garden is never a good choice for those who try their hand at self-production the first few times. Spending a few extra euros to buy high-performance substrates is a good choice for anyone who wants to get the most out of a crop without running into problems that would put any crop at risk. Remember, there is nothing more natural than growing a plant directly into the ground! Normally the potting soils that are sold in grow shops are all highly suitable for growing cannabis. In fact, the best brands of fertilizers also produce a large part of their own substrates, already pre-fertilized with the addition of perlite and full of trace elements, not to mention an N-P-K-ratio suitable for the various stages of cultivation.

A good mould is rich of peat and soft to the touch, favours the drainage of the water also thanks to the addition of vermiculite and is very porous, in order to allow a good rooting of the roots and favour the passage of air. There are more or less fertilised substrates on the market, it is up to the grower to choose the right growing medium according to his needs.

Strong roots for a good harvest

One of the most important factors to understand how well a plant will grow and how much it can produce is the health and strength of its root system. Below the surface of the growing medium, there is an intricate network of roots that stores sugars and starches (cannabis food) and transports the minerals needed by the plant. The roots of marijuana plants are covered with millions of small hairs that absorb water and minerals from the surrounding soil.

This root system sends minerals through the body of the plant to the leaves for use during photosynthesis, which in turn makes the starches and sugars the plant uses for food and energy. The larger and more extensive the root system, the better the plant's growth will be.

In the root system, humidity, temperature and oxygen levels directly affect growth. It is very important to remember that oxygen is essential for the roots, while the rest of the plant uses carbon dioxide (CO_2). When growing in pots, the best containers to house the plants are the most breathable or permeable to air, so that oxygen can easily enter the root zone.

The container before the contents

Let's not forget that first of all we need a good pot, for a respectable outdoor cultivation, we will choose it according to the size we want our plant to reach, the smaller the pot the more discreet our cultivation will be. Using medium sized pots is a good choice to optimize production and hide from prying eyes, and those ranging from 5 to 10 litres are a good solution.

Fertilization, organic or mineral?

Each nutrient company recommends a feeding cycle with different dosages and this only leads to confusion. This is because each company bases its own dosages and the resulting fertilization schedule for an entire line of single-brand products.

Let's be clear: the nutrients that the plant uses derive from the solubilization of the soil minerals and the recycling of the organic substances of dead organisms that are again mineralized by bacteria and other microorganisms. Fertilisation consists of providing the same elements in mineral form (chemical fertilisation) or as an organic substance to be decomposed (organic fertilisation). The final products of decomposition of the materials supplied with organic fertilisation are the same, the difference between the two techniques is ecological rather than chemical.

So, we have dusted off some basic notions to prepare a soil for a small outdoor self-production. We resort to this form of civil disobedience sparingly and without any pretension, where the State does not allow us access by legal means to a flower that is too often demonised. Although it is not legal, we must remind everyone that self-handling is the only solution to curb the monopoly of the narco-mafia, which makes money off simple consumers and damages public health, undermining the very authority of the State which is, in this context, their best accomplice.

CHAPTER 3 – Soil vs Hydroponics

Cannabis, like every other plant, has adapted its existence to the various growing environments, different for climate and soil, with modifications in the development, in order to make the most of the characteristics of the environment in which it is found. The selection made by human beings of certain individuals (cannabis) compared to others has been made for the particular types of use of the plant (especially fibre and resin) and for its yield possibilities in a particular environment. Traditionally, in countries with an equatorial or tropical climate, I the quantity and quality of the resin produced has favoured its use as a psychoactive plant; while in countries with a temperate climate, I the selection of varieties has been favoured for the maximum production of high quality textile fibre Ì (without paying too much attention to the resin content). The last century saw the beginning of the prohibition and persecution wanted by the United States (the tiny one is for contempt) against this extraordinary plant, prohibition and persecution extended all over the world and that still continue with fury, especially in countries where citizens are not considered able (or not wanted) to make responsible choices, like the country where we are.

The reasons for banning Cannabis have always been a bunch of lies, often contradictory to each other and often to refer to other substances. Persecution by governments, often forced to accept a ban on the cultivation of cannabis for any use, has created unnecessary social unease and led a section of the population to refuse to accept an unfair ban aimed at monopolistic interests.

The persecution of people who intended (and still intend to) use Cannabis has caused them to take precautions for their own safety, and to grow Cannabis trying to hide it from 'power'. In a closed environment, the possibilities of being seen are enormously reduced. Indoor cultivation, with artificial light, has high costs and the only convenient productions can be those of female inflorescences with a high percentage of resin for medicinal, health or recreational purposes, and the production of cuttings and selected seeds. In addition to research work applied to the study of the plant.

Indoor cultivation was therefore born to defend against prohibition, but it was soon realised that it offered numerous advantages:

- First, the lower risk of plants being seen by those who shouldn't.
- People living in an urban centre often do not even have a handkerchief or a sunny place; the air is impregnated with harmful substances, both for humans and plants; sunlight is confused with electric lighting. The possibility of setting up a closed environment in which plants can grow without any problems is definitely worth considering here.
- The big advantage is that it does not depend on the seasons: you can sow, cuttings and harvest ripe inflorescences at any time of the year.
- The harvest will no longer be just one, but during the year you can have from a minimum of three to five to six harvests.
- The time needed to create and stabilize new varieties can be very short.
- The genetic patrimony of the seeds obtained can be safe, while outdoors there is always the possibility that the wind may bring pollen of unknown origin.

- The environment is totally controlled. This means being able to guarantee optimal conditions for plants in every moment of their development. The quality may be higher than a plant that has had to go through a season that is sometimes unfavourable or adversity of any kind.

It should be added that with the study of Cannabis growth indoors, we have quickly understood what the plant needs for a particular production. This knowledge, applied to a good degree of sensibility and knowledge of the environment, could today bring the best results for productions in open field, economically much more profitable and potentially much healthier and respectful of the environment.

If it were possible to grow Cannabis without being persecuted, in the wild the growth elements of our plants might not be as perfectly balanced as we might think we could achieve indoors, but they would be freely available, differently for each growing location and different every season. It is precisely from diversity that the improvements of the species are created.

The same qualities cultivated indoors, if followed with care and with a suitable climate, have always proved to be better outdoors (no longer strong, better). Cannabis has a very complex genetic heritage, and each variety, if introduced in a particular environment, adapts to different conditions within a few generations, creating new phenotypes, different from the original variety. If there were not this useless, stupid and so harmful prohibition, a particular variety could develop in every particular microclimate (there are unfortunately less and less of them: traditional varieties, with a unique genetic heritage and developed after long selections, are disappearing rapidly: either for governmental campaigns of destruction or to be replaced by varieties with higher yields, but of different quality).

By genetic diversity, the possibilities of using this miraculous plant could certainly be further increased... but it is still considered criminal if you have more than one gram of THC! Although Cannabis grown indoors may have organoleptic characteristics superior to most outdoor crops, for me it remains a fallback. Hemp would be, and is, happy to be able to grow in full sun, in front of everyone's eyes and without being shamed by so many lies about it.

CHAPTER 4 - Marijuana in Hydroponics

Hydroponics is a method of growing plants and in this specific case a method for growing cannabis in a solution of water and nutrients.

As the name suggests, hydroponics is an above-ground growing method that uses water as the primary substrate. In a hydroponic plant, cannabis plants are grown in buckets or baskets filled with an inert growing medium and suspended on a reservoir full of water. The water contains all the nutrients necessary for the survival and growth of the plants, while the use of porous stones allows the tank to be oxygenated. This basic model comes in different forms and systems and the choice of planting depends on the preferences of each grower. There are many advantages to growing hydroponically and, in this article, we will try to cover them all. First, though, let's go into the history of this fascinating art form.

THE HISTORY OF HYDROPONICS

At first glance, hydroponics may seem to be the result of the most modern technological advances. However, this could not be further from the truth.

The origins of water crops date back thousands of years in human history. It is theorized that the famous roof gardens of Babylon, created in 600 B.C., made use of the principles of hydroponics. The region near the Euphrates was by nature dry and arid and it is assumed that the crops in these gardens could be fed by a leaching system that drew water from the river.

Advancing in time until the 10th and 11th centuries, the Aztec civilization made use of hydroponic cultivation to ensure the livelihood of their society. After being forced to leave its lands because of a conflict, this population settled along the shores of Lake Tenochtitlan. Here they began to build floating rafts covered with soil, allowing the plants to grow on the mantle and the roots to spread into the waters below.

More recently, but still far from the present day, we find the example of hydroponic cultivation by the English scientist John Woodward in 1699. His work consisted of growing green mint plants in water. This is how he discovered that plant species tend to grow faster in a water source mixed with soil.

The history of hydroponics has shown how effective this method can be in the most diverse environments and scenarios, including cannabis cultivation. Let's analyse the advantages of this interesting method and see how to apply it to grow high quality marijuana.

Hydroponics Growing: For & Against

Using a hydroponic system to grow Cannabis is the best way to raise your crop knowledge to a higher level, the important thing is to make sure you know what its advantages and disadvantages are.

ADVANTAGES OF HYDROPONIC CANNABIS CULTIVATION

- Increased production yields

Hydroponics allows much more abundant yields in smaller spaces, increasing the relationship between growing space and final harvest. This allows more experienced growers and commercial growers to achieve higher yields and, therefore, higher economic inputs.

- Optimum quality control

Hydroponic growing systems allow the quality and development of Cannabis plants to be kept under constant control. This allows to obtain a higher quality of the produced buds, compared to what can be obtained by growing them in soil.

- It is a much faster system

Cannabis grown with a hydroponic system matures much faster. This means that harvest times will be much shorter, allowing you to move on to a new crop more quickly. It is quite normal to talk about 6 harvests per year when using a hydroponic system.

- Fewer pests, fewer diseases

Since no organic substrates are involved, most pests and diseases, which find their natural habitat in the soil, do not create particular problems in this type of cultivation technique.

- Therefore, the use of pesticides is not necessary.

Reducing the risk of possible pest infestation means that there is no or almost no reason to use pesticides and, therefore, the quality of the final harvest will be higher.

- Less stress

When a hydroponic system is properly monitored, the possibility of plants suffering from water stress is much less frequent than with soil cultivation. In fact, we are considering a cultivation technique that only uses water as the main means of cultivation.

- More efficient

Cannabis plants grown using a hydroponic system make the best use of the water and fertilizers supplied to them, compared to growing on land. This means that not only will it be possible to achieve better results, but there will also no longer be a need for large quantities of nutrients.

- A much more precise method

Hydroponic systems offer a much more efficient control, thus succeeding in adopting a fertilization program much more targeted to the needs of each individual variety or plant. This step obviously requires a lot of practice, but it offers the most experienced grower's enormous advantages.

DISADVANTAGES OF HYDROPONIC CANNABIS CULTIVATION

- Different cultivation skills and knowledge are required

The main disadvantage when deciding to adopt a hydroponic system is that most of the above-mentioned advantages have no basis without a good knowledge and cultivation skills in this field. However, once you learn the strategies of hydroponic growing, the quality of your Cannabis plants will go to a higher level, but you need a lot of patience and practice to get there.

- It is not cheap

A functional hydroponic system is not cheap and the initial investment may discourage most people who grow as a hobby (especially when compared to the costs and benefits that can be obtained from growing on land).

- Hygiene is the key

Although the danger of disease is minimized, it can occur much faster in a hydroponic system. A disease of a plant with the root system constantly submerged in water can spread like wildfire and once it enters the hydroponic circuit, it will be much more difficult to eliminate. It is therefore necessary to always keep all materials as sterile and clean as possible, especially when using an open-air hydroponic system.

As you may have observed, hydroponics offers many advantages, but it requires special skills, a lot of patience and considerable capital to invest. If you are thinking of taking the big step, make sure you know all the steps you need to take to grow cannabis in a hydroponic system and have considerable capital to invest before you do the research. Once you understand the tricks of this technique, you will be rewarded like kings. First, however, you will have to overcome these initial obstacles.

Materials needed for a DIY hydroponic system

LIST

Here's what you'll need:

1. Lamps (LED or sodium)
2. Supports for lamps
3. Tent of cultivation
4. Tray and reservoir for hydroponic system
5. Porous stone and pump
6. Growing substrate (coconut fibre)
7. Mesh weave vases
8. Seeds
9. Ventilation fans and ducting pipes
10. Carbon filter
11. Oscillating fans
12. Nutrients for hydroponics
13. pH and PPM meter
14. Hygrometer

WHAT'S A SUBSTRATE?

Anyone who chooses to grow with hydroponics must think carefully about the substrate they intend to use. The most common types are coconut fibre, rock wool, expanded clay, various types of turf, lava stones, perlite and vermiculite. Obviously, it is important to choose the type that best suits the needs of our growing system. But one question arises, do we really need a substrate? What does the substrate actually do? How does it really work?

There is a misconception among growers that the function of the substrate only has to do with the relationship between air and water of the plant root. In reality the role of the substrate is only responsible for 15% of the plant's growth, the other 85% is in the hands of the grower.

The substrate is a medium in which the plant grows. It is mainly a single material, sometimes a combination of materials, which manage the substrate and aeration by holding and distributing water for the plant. In fact, as far as the plant is concerned, the substrate must contain water, oxygen and nutrients, drain everything correctly and remain neutral, so as not to interfere with the development of the plant. For the grower, the substrate must have a number of other factors: it must be reliable, economical to use and light. It must also be easy to process and dispose of. Ideally it should be non-polluting and biodegradable. And if you are a perfectionist, it should also be totally natural.

Hydroponics do not have a reservoir of nutrients that plant roots will absorb, but they are totally inert, so it will be the grower's job to prepare a nutrient solution to feed the plants. So, the substrate is just a support for the plant to develop an efficient root system with which it can absorb the nutrients supplied through the irrigation water.

One of the main advantages of using inert substrates is that you have full control over the nutrients the plants receive, it is the farmer who has to make the right nutrient mix for each stage of crop development. Normally, hydroponic growing media causes great oxygenation in the root zone, which means more roots and better developed (as we will see later, this also depends on the temperature of the irrigation water).

Traditionally, media such as gravel, washed sand, volcanic rock or perlite have often been used in hydroponics. Although many of these traditional media are still in use, new hydroponic growing media have appeared in recent decades.

Here are some of the most popular today:

Expanded clay, is one of the most popular means of hydroponics among growers. It provides good support for the roots of plants, with plenty of oxygen available, so that they grow significantly in cases of risk. If we want to avoid long and tedious work then it would be best to acquire this clay already thoroughly washed and with a pH adjusted to a value suitable for growing.

Rockwool (rockwool) is also one of the most widely used media in both hydroponic cultivation and construction, as it is an excellent thermal insulator. It was discovered at the beginning of the 20th century in Hawaii thanks to the volcanic activity in the area, and since then it has been produced from volcanic rock, emulating the action of a volcano on rocks. Its filamentous structure and high capacity air retention make it a widely used medium in agriculture.

Coconut fibre, which comes mainly from Asia, has become a very popular medium in recent decades. Its earth-like structure and its high capacity for water retention and oxygenation make coconut the preferred substrate of many farmers. It is often used to improve soils, and nowadays many commercial substrates have a share of coconut fibre to improve their consistency and properties. I recommend reading the post about growing marijuana in coconut fibre.

Perlite is a product derived from minerals that have been subjected to high temperatures to expand (as is also the case with expanded clay). It is often used to improve other substrates, although it can be used as a hydroponic growing medium through increased water retention and aeration.

Mapito is a medium used for years mainly by Dutch growers. It is a mixture of rockwool and coconut flakes with a high oxygen and moisture retention capacity, ideal for growing marijuana. It is used a lot like rockwool.

Hydroponics systems

Hydro / aeroponic cultivation systems work great with most marijuana varieties. Due to its characteristics and needs, this plant adapts very well to such systems, grows vigorously and flowers beautifully if the irrigation parameters are correct.

If we have decided to go into hydroponics, we have mainly two options: buy a finished product that only requires that we mount it and plug it in or make our own. Although it may seem like a challenge for the novice cannabis grower, anyone with some experience with hydroponics could easily make their own system without spending too much money.

There are many hydroponic operating systems with small variations. These are some of the most commonly used:

Passive systems based on the capillarity of the medium surrounding the roots and where no type of pump is used to provide the nutrient solution. The medium remains in contact with the nutrient solution stored in a small reservoir.

Flow and reflow systems use a pump to fill the tray in which the systems are housed, so that the root area is also completely immersed. Once the immersion is complete, the nutrient solution is drained to the reservoir while waiting for the next irrigation.

Drip irrigation is one of the most widely used because of the ease of installation, maintenance and excellent system results offered. A water pump transports the nutrient solution through a series of pipes and capillary irrigation from the reservoir to the plants. The frequency of irrigation is set according to the needs of the system depending on the state of development you are in.

In DWC systems, the roots hang from the netpot to the nutrient solution deposited in the bottom of the closed bucket that serves as a pot. An air pump constantly oxygenates the nutrient solution producing hundreds of micro-bubbles and splashes, which feed the plant roots.

NFT systems consist of a tray from which the nutrient solution flows slowly and on which the plants rest.

Thus, the plant roots are in permanent contact with the nutrients provided by the water. A water pump ensures that the nutrient solution circuit is not interrupted.

From this point different types of professional and domestic hydroponic growing systems have developed, sometimes combining some of those that have seen and obtaining hybrid systems with excellent performance.

There is another technique that simply does not use any type of medium. This method is also called aeroponics, and follows the same principle as the hydroponic growing system: feeding the plants through a nutrient solution and not from the medium.

In aeroponics, the roots hang freely inside a dark chamber, where they receive large amounts of nutrients and oxygen needed for growth. Based on this idea, we have developed numerous aeroponic growing systems with small variations, or systems that could be considered hybrids such as the already mentioned NFT (Nutrient Film Technique) or DWC (Deep water culture), which then result in a mix between hydroponics (the roots live in a medium, the nutrient solution) and aeroponics (part of the roots hang without the medium).

What are aeroponics and hydroponics?

But what are aeroponics and hydroponics? Have you ever seen a cultivation system that sprays the feed solution as if it were a thin mist compared to the root feed system? This is an aeroponic system, a technique by which water and nutrients are delivered through a high-pressure nozzle. This technique is not widely used in its pure form. Although some companies like to call their systems "aeroponic", such installations are normally only seen in research institutes and universities.

AEROPONICS

Aeroponics has its advantages and disadvantages. It saturates the oxygen supply solution, giving the roots a very healthy environment, and the most interesting application is its use in plant breeding. But if you want to keep the plant until it is mature you will notice that the main area develops too quickly and too abundantly, to the detriment of the air-based part of the plant.

This is not normally what we grow for - cannabis is not a root vegetable. But even if you want to grow root vegetables it's not always practical, because with aeroponics, the roots tend to remain soft, unlike when they are constantly immersed in water and never develop the crunchy qualities we look for in a root, like liquorice root...

AERO-HYDROPONICS

Aero-hydroponics is a modification of aeroponics. It actually started in the mid 80's, in California, where Laurence Brooke decided to try to bring hydroponic aero-culture to the international market. She started with the "EGS" (Ein Gedi System), then a group developed it at the University of Davis, California, to study the oxygen level in water, which Brooke has transformed into the best propagation unit to date: the "Rainforest". This unit sprays water from a nozzle onto the roots, but not in the form of a mist, but more like a revolving spray.

These days there are many variations of the aero-hydroponic system on the market, some are effective, others less, depending on the experience and knowledge of the manufacturer. You can also build your own aero-hydroponic system with a little help from the many magazines and books that there are these days in hydroponic shops.

In aero-hydroponics water is saturated with oxygen by a number of methods: spraying, injection or cascade. These are usually based on a pump that compresses the water through different irrigation pipes and sprinklers before it falls back into the reservoir. A well-designed aero-hydroponic system must find the perfect balance between the different components and the correct proportions between the different water streams and the shapes of the different parts (pipes, tanks, sprinklers and irrigation devices).

Neither aeroponics nor aero-hydroponics need substrate (or very little). They just need a way to support the plants, usually in the form of small coconut pots, plastic nets or simple rubber rings. They only have water as substrate. Now all that is left is water and the grower.

One thing we know for sure is that the most difficult problem with the substrate has been eradicated, but you are probably wondering if you can find other problems that might be just as difficult To completely and safely rule out traditional substrates, you need to be absolutely sure of the water supply for the plant, have good management

for the air circulation and a neutral and clean environment. In aeroponics and aero-hydroponics this is the perfect basis: well oxygenated water for the roots and good drainage.

When this has been said is also done, for the rest, once again, it is all in the hands of the grower. You have to make sure you have a well-balanced solution, complete with nutrients; a perfect EC and pH, good ventilation, ideal temperature, good air humidity and hygienic working methods, just as if you were growing any other plant or with any other growing technique.

CHAPTER 5 - Hydroponic Growing of Cannabis

Growing marijuana with the hydroponic cultivation system is relatively simple. These are some of the basic principles you should remember:

Nutrients are supplied with irrigation water, so you need to acquire liquid nutrients (water-soluble or water-solid) prepared for this type of crop. Remembering water only with water in an inert environment means that the plant does not die from lack of moisture, but neither is nutrient.

The nutrient solution must contain the maximum amount of oxygen, and therefore should be at 19-22°C. When using a nutrient solution tank, therefore installing an air pump to oxygenate is highly recommended. Its acidity should be between pH 5.5 (growth) and pH 6 (flowering). The approximate EC (amount of nutrients dissolved in water) should vary between 1-1.2 (growth) and 1.4-1.8 (flowering).

When using nutrient solution reservoir, it should be emptied and cleaned approximately every two weeks. For best results, install an air pump to oxygenate the nutrient solution and a water heater to keep it at a suitable temperature of approximately 20°C. Of course, it is also necessary to have a water pump to provide the solution for the plants. Finally, a water thermometer allows you to know the temperature of the solution at all times.

The frequency of irrigation will depend largely on the chosen substrate and the development phase of the plant. The experienced grower will not have too many problems adapting to the needs of the plants, although the beginner grower should carefully observe the state of the substrate to know when to irrigate. Once the characteristics of the substrate in relation to the water needs of the plant are known, the watering frequency program becomes an easy and mechanical process.

THE COSTS OF HYDROPONICS

When we talk about hydroponics, images of high-tech systems immediately come to mind: automatic switches, flashing lights, timers and chronometers. In reality, the cost of a hydroponic system depends mainly on the amount of money you are willing to invest. There are various types of hydroponic systems, from the very simple ones consisting of a simple plastic bucket, to self-draining systems with automatic irrigation. To save time, buy a low-cost hydroponics starter kit. In it you will find all the material you need to tackle every stage of plant growth, from germination to ripening. One kit cost about $250.

Choose a hydroponics plant

All systems are similar in that they use a nutrient-enriched aqueous solution. However, systems can vary greatly depending on certain factors, such as exposure and water circulation. Most of the following systems can be purchased commercially, but if you are skilled in DIY, you can easily build one using buckets, drills, pumps and porous stones.

DEEP WATER CULTURE

Deep Water Culture is a good starting point for beginners and probably the cheapest option. The plants are placed in buckets filled with a nutrient solution and an air pump that constantly provides oxygen.

EBB AND FLOW

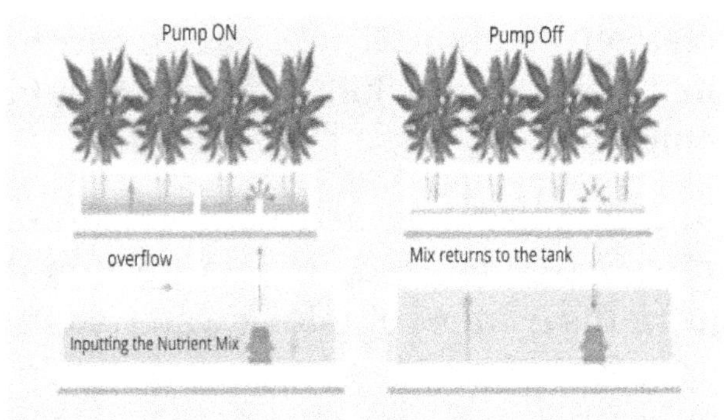

A system of ebb and flow (also known as "tide table") consists, in fact, in making the water flow and reflux. These systems are composed of numerous buckets suspended on a tray with an inlet and an outlet for water. Both openings are connected to an external tank containing nutrients, a porous stone to oxygenate the water supply and a pump to move the water in the tray. In these hydroponic systems, the roots are not constantly immersed in the water, but rather the water periodically floods the tray with fresh oxygen and nutrient-enriched water. At the end of the pumping cycle, all the water returns to the external reservoir.

This system allows for periodic fertilisation of the plants. The time interval in which the tray is empty allows growers to take care of the roots and harvest the plants more easily.

DROP BY DROP SYSTEM

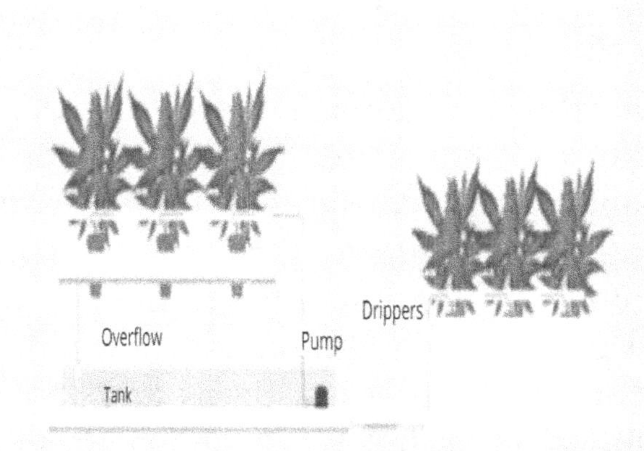

The drop by drop system installed in a hydroponic system is very similar to the one used to irrigate soil crops. It consists of a large tray full of substrate, such as expanded clay. The plants are placed directly into the substrate, and each one is irrigated by its own drip pipe located in the immediate vicinity. An external water tank with porous stones and pump provides constant water dripping on each plant. The roots are continuously exposed to air, and excess water drips down the substrate and back into the outer reservoir.

NUTRIENT FILM TECHNIQUE

If Deep Water Culture is the equivalent of growing cannabis plants in an artificial lake, then the nutrient film technique is the equivalent of growing grass on a river. This system consists of placing the plants in an inclined cylinder, so that water can enter from one side and exit from the other by gravity. The roots grow in the cylinder, where they are exposed to running water. The water enters from a reservoir in which a porous stone and a pump are immersed, and then comes back again once the cycle is complete.

WICK SYSTEM

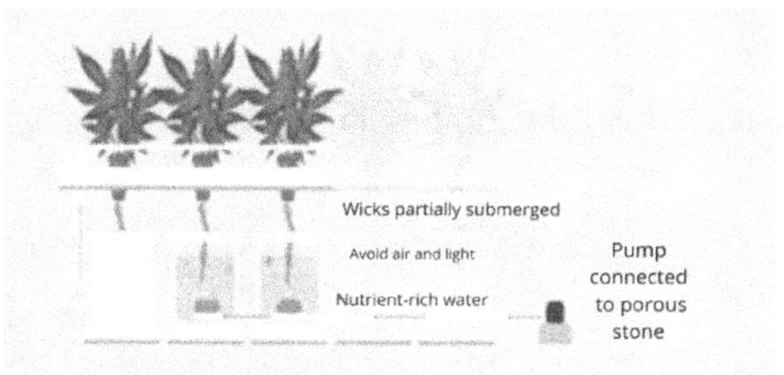

The wick system is a basic hydroponic configuration using a tray similar to the drop system filled with expanded clay. Underneath the tray there is a water deposit, from which numerous wicks come out and enter the growing medium. The water moves along the wicks and passively hydrates the substrate. No pump is required for this system.

AEROPONICS

The water is atomised and dispersed in the air to optimise aeration and hydration. The plants are placed in the upper part of a large tank, filled with 25% water. A pump is immersed in the water, which pushes the solution towards water diffusers positioned below the root systems. This thin mist is constantly absorbed by the roots, allowing the plants to receive huge quantities of air and water at the same time.

How to prepare a hydroponic system

Once you have chosen the system best suited to your needs, you must prepare it correctly to avoid potentially harmful situations. The wet and dark nature of the water tanks is an ideal habitat for different families of pathogens. Before using the system, sterilize all equipment to minimize the risk of contamination. Thoroughly clean buckets, trays, pipes and tanks with alcohol, hot water and hydrogen peroxide. Once sterilized, you can proceed by following the instructions to configure it correctly.

ENSURE REGULAR MAINTENANCE OF THE SYSTEM

All hydroponic systems require frequent maintenance to ensure the optimal growth environment. Below are the main factors you should consider.

A) ALWAYS MONITOR THE PH

To ensure an optimal growth environment you will need to constantly test the pH value. Nutrients are more available to plants when the environment is slightly acidic. Therefore, a pH of 5.5-5.8 is required. Use a pH test kit to test the pH regularly and be sure to replace the solution every week in order to maintain this range. During flowering, plants prefer a pH of 6.

B) KEEP THE WATER TEMPERATURE AT ABOUT 20°C.

Hydroponically grown cannabis prefers temperatures of 20°C. This parameter can be monitored using a water thermometer and modified using a water heater if temperatures are too low.

(C) TO PROVIDE THE RIGHT AMOUNT OF FERTILIZER

Hydroponic plants require the same nutrients as their soil grown counterparts. The easiest way to fertilize plants is to buy hydroponically formulated fertilizers that contain all the substances needed for both the vegetative and flowering phases. Product labels also show how often they should be added and with what dilution.

(D) KEEP ALL EQUIPMENT CLEAN TO AVOID CONTAMINATION

Both tanks and trays must be emptied and cleaned about every two weeks. This process will keep the roots of the plants safe from invading pathogens and diseases. Repeat the same process mentioned in the section on plant preparation.

(E) SELECT A VARIETY TO BE GROWN HYDROPONICALLY

Variety selection is a very important factor in hydroponics. Plants grown indoors within these systems are free to absorb fertiliser extremely quickly, which often results in explosive and very rapid growth. For this reason, selecting a large sativa variety will not be the best choice, especially if your system is installed inside a grow cabinet.

Smaller, more compact varieties are best for indoor hydroponic systems. Starting with a small variety is advantageous for several reasons. First of all, it allows you to grow several plants in a smaller space, allowing for more diversity and potentially higher yields. Also, if the plants show a jolt of growth, there will still be enough room in the room to cope with sudden changes in height.

Below are two varieties that we recommend for hydroponic growing.

1 - WHITE WIDOW

White Widow is a perfectly balanced hybrid with genetics for 50% Indica and 50% sativa. It was created using a White Widow S1 and causes a well-balanced high that stimulates and excites the mind while relaxing and calming the body. THC concentrations of 19% ensure a powerful psychoactive experience lasting several hours. These inflorescences contain a terpenic profile that emanates earthy and pine flavours and smells.

The White Widow reaches a height of 60-100cm when grown indoors, making it a perfect candidate for the space requirements of a hydroponic operation. Expect excellent yields of 450-500g/m² after a flowering period of 8-9 weeks.

2 - ROYAL DWARF

The Royal Dwarf is another obvious option for an indoor hydroponic plant. This variety combines Skunk and ruderalis with the aim of creating a compact plant that offers excellent yields and moderate potency. Royal Dwarf is sativa-dominant and induces a motivating and stimulating cerebral high, fuelled by a THC level of 13%. Every mouthful of this marijuana is imbued with sweet flavours, accompanied by citric notes.

In indoor crops the plants reach low heights of 40-70cm, producing yields of up to 200g/m², and moving from seed to harvest in just 8 weeks.

CHAPTER 6 - Cleaning and Reusing Water from a Hydroponic System

Disinfecting and reusing water from a hydroponic system is a perfect way to reduce water consumption and maximize the yield of your grow room.

One of the main advantages of a hydroponic system is that it allows you to recycle and reuse water. Therefore, a hydroponic system can help us to reduce water consumption, respecting the environment and cutting costs.

However, recycling water in a hydroponic system can be complicated. The water used can carry bacteria, viruses and pathogens, which can infect the plantation. It is therefore essential to sterilise the water before using it again, so as to reduce the spread of diseases among plants.

PASTEURISATION

In the pasteurization process, heat is used to kill bacteria. It is widely used in the dairy industry to sanitize milk. Pasteurization can also be used to sterilize other liquids, including water for hydroponic systems.

During pasteurisation the water is heated quickly. Heat exchangers are used, designed to exchange heat energy between two fluids or gases. Without going into too much detail, an exchanger uses a fluid, or gas (called a heating/cooling agent) to heat/cool water in the hydroponic system.

One of the main advantages of pasteurization is that it is not necessary to pre-filter the water. This procedure minimizes the deposition of minerals and other biological agents in the water. Unfortunately, these agents can instead accumulate in the exchanger used for pasteurization. This means that the unit will have to be cleaned regularly in order to function properly.

OZONIZATION STERILIZATION

In ozone sterilization, water must be mixed with ozone (O_3), a natural gas present in high concentrations in the ozonosphere, where it is created by ultraviolet rays from the sun. Ozone can also be generated artificially, and used to sterilize and recycle water from hydroponic systems.

For ozonisation, ozone generators are used to create the gas in the grow room. There are two types of generators (corona discharge and ultraviolet). Both separate the molecules of O_2 into individual oxygen atoms. The atoms quickly bind to O_2 molecules to create ozone (O_3). It is then injected into the water to remove any contaminants.

Ozonisation has several advantages. It is by far the most effective sterilization method for water, and acts quickly on any contamination. It is also environmentally friendly, and the use of this system in the grow room can prevent the appearance of diseases and pests on plants (including mites and red spiders). However, ozonisation is an expensive procedure. Ozone is also very corrosive. If used improperly, it can damage your plant.

UV STERILIZATION

UV disinfection is another very safe way to clean and recycle water from a hydroponic system. It does not involve the use of chemicals, and is therefore very suitable for those who want to cultivate in a natural and ecological way.

To sterilize with ultraviolet rays, it is necessary to pass water through a radiation chamber, containing high pressure UV lamps. The UV rays from the lamps penetrate the molecules present in the water (such as bacteria and pathogens), destroying their DNA. At high doses, UV rays can also remove chlorine from water (a process called photolysis). UV radiation is often used to purify water for domestic use, as in the case of the Catskill-Delaware Water Ultraviolet Disinfection Facility in New York (USA), the facility that sterilizes drinking water in New York.

Compared to pasteurization and ozonisation, UV sterilization is cost-effective. In addition, it is totally natural and does not generate hazardous residues. The disadvantage of UV disinfection is that it cannot remove dissolved organic substances, chemical contaminants or inorganic compounds from the water. Therefore, at standard dosages it cannot remove heavy metals, salts, or chlorine (higher amounts of UV are required for photolysis).

How to choose the method of water sterilization

All the purification methods we have illustrated in this article offer several benefits. However, each of them also has limitations. The choice of one sterilization method over another depends on personal needs, budget, availability of equipment in your area, and the size of the plantation.

If you want to minimize costs, UV sterilization is probably the best choice. Ozone generators and pasteurization machines are quite expensive. In addition, they require constant maintenance, which affects the overall costs of the entire operation. Ultraviolet radiation chambers, on the other hand, are cheaper to buy and operate in the long term. They are therefore perfect for those on a limited budget.

UV and ozone sterilization are ideal for large-scale cultivation. Pasteurization is much more expensive, suitable for those with a small plantation and a larger budget. Ozonisation offers the best results, because ozone is a very powerful disinfectant. Remember, however, that it can be corrosive and should be handled with the utmost care.

CHAPTER 7 - Older Cannabis Varieties

An indigenous variety can be defined as a variety of Cannabis grown in the wild, in a wild environment, developed within a specific geographical region. Over the centuries, these isolated varieties have begun to develop specific qualities in order to adapt and, therefore, survive the regions they colonize. These particular varieties almost always take their name from their area of origin, terms that we often find as suffixes in hybrid varieties descended from them.

In the '70s and '80s, some of the most passionate Cannabis enthusiasts began to travel the world in search of new native varieties, to be later included in their crops. These varieties are also nicknamed 'relics', genetics that over the years spread to different parts of the world, such as California and Europe.

Recently, Arjan Roskam, the founder of Greenhouse Seeds, based in Amsterdam, has been attracting worldwide attention for his project "Strain Hunters", the variety hunters, real documentaries about their travels. The Strainhunters, his colleague, travel all over the world in search of native varieties, the most authentic, to preserve their original genetic biodiversity, in order to subsequently create new hybrid varieties. The biodiversity of a variety is very important in the field of research, especially for its ability to adapt and survive in the most hostile environments.

The different climatic areas of our planet have created varieties with the most peculiar aspects and the most diverse cannabinoid composition (even if belonging to the same family and with minimal differences from a botanical point of view).

Cannabis Sativa

The native Cannabis sativa comes from areas of Asia, Anatolia and North Africa. These varieties tend to become much taller (up to 3-4 meters) and slimmer than their Indica cousins. Similarly, their internodal distance is greater and the flower cluster structure is more elongated and less compact, requiring significantly longer flowering periods. The leaves appear thinner, with the indentation of the leaf blades much more pronounced. The flower aroma of a Sativa plant is often described as a fruity, floral fragrance. Native Cannabis sativa varieties have managed to adapt to climate zones close to the equator, characterised by long summers and intense sunlight, but have lost the ability to properly complete flowering at latitudes slightly to the north or south of their original latitudes. Some of the world's best-known Sativa varieties include Thai, Acapulco Gold, Durban Poison and Panama Red.

Cannabis Indica

The native varieties of Cannabis Indica originate in the mountainous regions of Afghanistan, Pakistan and India. Indica genetics result in much smaller (reaching a maximum height of 2 metres) and bushy plants with a more exuberant resin production than their Sativa cousins. Indica varieties complete their flowering period in a shorter time, demonstrating a rather low elongation during the flowering phase. Indica leaves appear stompier, with much less indentation in the leaf blade. The bunches of flowers that develop from these plants are much more compact and heavy. The aroma emanating from the buds of Indica varieties is often described as musky and earthy. These genetics has managed to adapt quite well even to crops at milder, northernmost latitudes. Two of the most famous Indica varieties are Hindu Kush and Afghani.

Cannabis Ruderalis

Cannabis ruderalis is a particular variety that originates in Eastern Europe, the Himalayas and Siberia. Cannabis ruderalis is not only the smallest member of the Cannabis family, reaching a maximum height of one meter, but it is also the least potent variety in terms of cannabinoid concentration. However, the characteristic that has made it so exceptional is its ability to switch to flowering without having to wait for the change of the photoperiod, i.e. the hours of light received. This property is due to the forced adaptation developed in areas with a harsh climate, at extreme northern and southern latitudes. In these regions, summer days can reach 20 hours of sunlight, but the duration of this season is extremely short. The most experienced researchers and growers have used this genetic characteristic to create the auto-flowering varieties that we all know today. Thanks to this property of theirs, it is possible to harvest the buds of a plant just 60 days after germination, making it possible to obtain two or more harvests per season in the most temperate climates.

The 5 Oldest Cannabis Varieties

Now that you have understood what native cannabis varieties are, we can start to analyse some of these ancient plants in detail. The interesting fact is that only very few of these strains have become the pillars of the thousands of genetics that exist today.

AFGHANI

The origin of the Afghani strain is quite obvious. This is one of the most recognizable native varieties. True to its Indica origins, it generates a persistent high and a pleasant sense of heaviness that nails the consumer to the sofa. This sensation matches perfectly with the sweet, skunk and spicy aromas emanating from the buds.

Afghani and Afghani 1 feminized seeds are definitely recommended to all fans of this enchanting Indica strain. These plants are famous for their small and easily manageable size. Despite their short stature, they offer abundant yields. After tasting the dense and compact buds, you will

become a fervent supporter of Afghani for life.

THAI

Unlike previous genetics, Thai is pure sativa. It generates a cerebral and energizing high. That's why it's ideal to consume as soon as you wake up. In addition, its effects are often creative and stimulating. All in all, this variety is ideal for the most productive consumers. But avoid smoking it in the evening, unless you plan to stay up all night.

We have a couple of excellent varieties available, which are descended from these legendary genetics. Thai Fantasy is very easy to grow outdoors. Thanks to its robust and vigorous nature, it can withstand even the most adverse weather conditions. AK-420 is a productive and very solid plant, perfect for beginner growers.

NEPALESE

The term Nepalese is generally used to refer to any variety originating in the region of Nepal, including the country itself and surrounding areas. This particular environment has inoculated Nepalese plants with very earthy aromas and a slight sweet berry flavour. These varieties are known for their relaxing and comforting effects, typical of Indica. However, their growth style is predominantly satirical.

The extraordinary Nepal Jam raises the entire Nepalese strain to a higher level. It is a 100% sativa variety. It can produce full-bodied and tasty buds both indoors and outdoors. If you are looking for genetics with a little more power, Vision Cookies is the plant for you. Its flowers contain 20% THC and, thanks to 70% Indica genes, will nail you to the couch hard.

HINDU KUSH

This indigenous strain descends from the mountain ranges of the same name, and is one of the most famous genetics in the world. The Hindu Kush region stretches over 800km between Pakistan and Afghanistan. Here, the hostile climate has shaped vigorous, world-famous plants. You only need to take a mouthful of Hindu Kush to understand why this area is famous for its prized hashish. The aroma contains a mix of spices and nuances of musk, with an unmistakable fragrance of old-school hash.

Kush varieties usually cause very intense physical high, and a feeling of mental bliss. For therapeutic consumers, this genetic is a valuable aid against insomnia, depression and stress. Feminized Hindu Kush seeds contain all these positive effects, as well as a short flowering period. If you like to make hash or concentrates, you should definitely choose these seeds. If you are looking for a hybrid suitable for indoor growing, the best option is our Kalini Asia. This plant reaches a height of just one meter. It produces abundant buds of excellent quality. Thanks to 22% THC, this cross between Hindu Kush and Pure Purple Afghani will immediately win you over.

ACEH

From the hills of Aceh, an Indonesian province, comes this rare native, purely sativa variety. It releases wonderful sweet and tropical aromas, inherited from its exotic ancestors. Its vibrant, sugary and earthy taste will activate psychoactive effects in no time. Aceh is a perfect variety to counter mood disorders. In fact, its high is cerebral and very euphoric. It's really hard to have sad or negative thoughts after you've tasted a mouthful of fine Aceh tops! In this variety the THC levels are below average (the buds produce about 10% THC). However, the effect is described as intense and energetic.

Like most native varieties, Aceh also shows a remarkable degree of flexibility. The specimens have managed to adapt to the warm and humid climate of this region. Therefore, strains derived from this genetics can be harvested after less than 10 weeks of flowering.

Indica vs Sativa

Today it is widely accepted that marijuana occurs in two different species: Cannabis Indica and Cannabis sativa. The crossing of these two types has led to a large variety of hybrid strains with unique characteristics.

A mention should be made of hemp, a nomenclature that indicates the male cannabis sativa plant. When we refer to marijuana, however, we consider the inflorescences of the female plant.

The differences between Indica and sativa marijuana remain a topic of enormous and open discussion, especially among scientists who study the plant. However, most of them agree that Indica and sativa are two plants that differ in various ways.

APPEARANCE OF MARIJUANA TYPES

The most common way to distinguish cannabis Indica from cannabis sativa is appearance, or what scientists call morphology.

Sativa cannabis is a tall, vaguely branched plant with long, narrow leaves. They are usually grown outdoors and can reach galactic heights (5 meters). Amazing. Real trees.

Indica marijuana plants are shorter, densely branched and have wider leaves. These plants are more suitable for indoor growing.

EFFECTS

In addition to having different aspects, Indica and Sativa marijuana are plants that have different effects on different people, but more generally have the following distinctions:

Sativa marijuana

Reviving and energetic. Awakening and Creative.

Cerebral, spatial, rainy and sometimes hallucinogenic travel.

More suitable for daytime use

Indica Marijuana

Relaxing and soothing. Sofa.

Tingling or tingling of certain parts of the body and extreme muscle relaxation.

More suitable for night-time use.

However, no scientific study has confirmed these differences. In fact, the story suggests a much simpler difference between the two types of marijuana: Indica and sativa.

The initial classification of Indica marijuana was made by French biologist Jean-Baptiste Lamarck in 1785.

Lamarck observed that the traditional hemp crops present in Europe did not show alterations in mind due to use, compared to some varieties found in India and from which hashish was made.

He then coined the term Cannabis Indica to distinguish Indian Marijuana from European Marijuana, currently known as Cannabis Sativa. Similarly, Cannabis Indica was then recognized as a therapeutic drug by Western medicine during the 1800s.

GENETIC DIFFERENCES

Scientists who have studied the differences between Indica and sativa have created a number of theories based on genetics. One prevalent theory focuses on the genetic production of THC and CBD.

Plants that produce high levels of THC express genes that code for the synthesis of the THCA enzyme. This enzyme converts CBG to THCA, which becomes THC when heated (try also reading how to decarboxylate marijuana to understand how THC is released only by heating).

These plants are generally considered sativa.

On the other hand, some plants express genes that code for the synthesis of the CBDA enzyme. This enzyme converts CBG to CBDA, the precursor of CBD. These plants are generally considered Indica.

According to this explanation, Sativa marijuana has much more THC than CBD, while Indica marijuana has higher levels of CBD.

The problem is that many strains today produce varying amounts of both enzymes. Some researchers believe that this is due to hybridisation.

An alternative theory based on geographical origin has also been proposed.

Recent attempts to distinguish Sativa Marijuana from Indica Marijuana have been based on genetic and geographical theories. There are also some lesser known species, such as Cannabis Ruderalis, which is typical of the regions of Eastern Europe, Mongolia and Russia. The latter is widely used to create Indica and Sativa-dominant hybrids, exploiting the resistance of Ruderalis.

CHAPTER 8 - Cannabis Hybrids

Cannabis, like any other plant, can be purebred or a hybrid blend of several varieties. Since the industry started marketing it, both pure varieties and existing hybrids are continuously mixed and remixed. These new plants are known as hybrids.

The hybrids are the result of a human attempt to customise plants with specific characteristics, normally found in ruderalis, sativa and Indica varieties. The most valuable hybrids are those that inherit the best qualities from their parents.

WHAT TYPES OF HYBRIDS EXIST?

Normally, there are four types of hybrid varieties:

- **Sativa x sativa**: Two different sativa varieties are crossed together.
- **Indica x Indica**: Two different Indica varieties are crossed together.
- **Sativa x Indica**: The varieties described with this abbreviation show mainly sativa characteristics. However, you can still see traits of both cannabis genetics. For example, a plant of this type could become tall with purple buds.
- **Indica x sativa**: This variety will express the characteristics of both, but the dominance will be Indica.

There are also auto-flowering hybrids, plants that at some point in their evolutionary process have been crossed with ruderalis genetics.

All plants require the same basic process to be hybridized and cannabis is no less. A female plant has to be fertilized from the pollen of a male plant. This is a completely natural phenomenon. However, for the creation of new crosses, breeders work on selective hybridization in controlled environments. In other words, they choose the female plant and the male plant to recreate one or more specific traits.

The seeds germinated by this process will be first generation hybrids of male and female parents. The plants that show the best traits will be crossed again. Once the desired results are obtained, the breeder will "stabilize" the new variety. In other words, they will cross a young hybrid with a close relative to strengthen the characteristics. This process is usually repeated over three or more generations to further stabilize the characteristics.

Cannabis reproduces "sexually" or "asexually". The sexual reproductive process involves a combination of different parents. Vegetative methods, however, also include cloning and even root splitting. Asexual reproduction makes it possible to produce the same identical plant several times.

Hybrids

As their name suggests, cannabis hybrid varieties are the result of a cross between pure genetics or other hybrids in a new variety. One of the first man-made hybrids is 'Skunk', the first famous cross between an Indica and sativa. But it's certainly not the only one.

Varieties are mainly hybridized for the following reasons:

Obtaining a specific cannabinoid content

Many hybrids are composed of a mixture of both sativa and Indica "parents". This allows the breeder to determine the type of impact the new variety will have. Do you want to reach the couch and never move again? Try a predominantly Indica variety. Are you looking for a little cerebral creativity? Try sativa-dominant varieties. You want an auto flowering strain? It's a hybrid of ruderalis and another variety. As medical research expands, more and more genetics are being created to ensure certain concentrations of specific cannabinoids. Many cannabis varieties maximise the THC or CBD content. Medical cannabis for children, for example, is hybridized by specific cannabis varieties characterized by low THC and high CBD concentrations.

Dimensions

Whether you grow indoors or outdoors, the choice of growing space may impose certain restrictions. Sauces become as big as trees. Indica's tend to look like small shrubs. However, hybrids can be selected for size, ability to take on a bushy structure and other characteristics. Some sativa hybrids, in other words, can even be confused with Indica varieties.

Auto flowering

These varieties are all crossed, at a certain point in their evolution, with a parent ruderalis. This means that your plants will flower regardless of the hours of light they are exposed to.

Resin

Some plants are more resinous than others. Hybrids are specifically crossed for their resin content. Indica tend to be more resinous than sativa, but even here hybrids can overturn the rules of the game.

Terpenes & flavonoids

Cannabis is proving to be a medicinal plant in its own right and the role of its essential oils is attracting increasing interest. Hybrids combining different essential oils have made their way onto the market, but they are still in their infancy.

Yields

The productivity of a plant depends on its inherited characteristics.

Resistance (and colour)

Some varieties of cannabis, especially Indica, come from areas of the planet characterized by cold temperatures and short days. The hybrids can be reworked to better tolerate these conditions and to develop purple colourations. Purple cannabis is the big favourite among the most popular varieties for connoisseurs. Today, these traits can be obtained without necessarily having to stress the plant with cold air during its growth.

Resistance to diseases and pests.

Just like humans, some varieties of cannabis are more resistant to their natural predators and the environment in which they grow.

Hybrids are not all created the same way

The development of a quality hybrid requires time and work. And not all hybrids are the same.

Variety existing only in the form of a clone

It is a variety that is kept alive to preserve certain characteristics. The grower can produce clones that are genetically identical to the mother plant and redistribute them. A clone is the only way to ensure that that exact genetic characteristic is preserved. However, the growing conditions will greatly influence the final product.

Genetically stable varieties

A breeder that selects both male and female plants will go so far as to hybridise the plants over and over again to stabilise certain characteristics. The seeds thus obtained will show those specific qualities each time they are planted. That said, there will always be some genetic variation.

Genetically unstable varieties

Although they can be produced faster than genetically stable seeds, their qualities are absolutely unpredictable. Renowned seed shops would never sell unstable genetically stable varieties.

CHAPTER 9 - Seeding Method

There are different techniques for germinating cannabis seeds. However, some of these methods involve risks, so we advise you to follow an alternative route. In this chapter, we will show you our preferred method of germination, and then move on to some less reliable techniques. We will also examine the process of transplanting freshly germinated seeds.

Germinate cannabis seeds directly into the substrate

For some strange reason, cannabis growers tend to complicate life unnecessarily when they have to germinate seeds by adopting complex and even risky techniques. You've probably already heard of germinating in damp paper towels or a glass of water (which we'll discuss later), but personally we believe that the simplest and most effective way to germinate a seed is directly in the growing medium.

Simply place the seed about 0.5cm deep into the soil and cover it slightly. Check the environment and keep it warm and humid - 20°C is the ideal temperature. Keep the medium moist, but do not saturate it - water saturated medium can do more harm than good. You can place a lamp over the seed to provide the proper temperature for germination. Your precious cannabis seed will germinate happily within a few days!

Keep in mind that your seeds do not need any nutrients, at least for the first two weeks of growth. Novice growers often make the wrong mistake by thinking that they will promote growth by adding nutrients at this early stage. DO NOT DO IT! The seed contains everything it needs to grow for a couple of weeks. Adding more nutrients can burn the seedling before it has even started growing. Feed your seedling with normal water, this will ensure the development of strong roots. If you really want, you can use a root stimulator even if it is not absolutely necessary.

From experience, we know that germinating seeds directly into the substrate is not only the simplest and most reliable technique, but also the safest method for your seeds. The other techniques require the transfer of freshly germinated seeds into a pot, so there is always a risk of damaging the young taproot in the movement manoeuvres. Other methods can even rot the seeds. Furthermore, we have not noticed any advantage in using these methods over direct germination in the substrate.

Germination kit

To further simplify the germination phase, we recommend using a germination kit. These kits have everything you need to give your seeds the best possible initial conditions.

The Smart Start includes 20 pots already filled with compost and a special mix of stimulators to improve germination, activating the microbial life of the soil. All you need to do is moisten the Smart Start jars on which you have distributed the Stimulator Mix sachet with water, plant the seeds in each jar and cover with soil. Then place the tray in a place at room temperature and make sure the soil remains moist (but not soaked). In a few days, your seeds will germinate. We recommend using the Smart Start in a mini greenhouse to create the ideal environment for seedling development.

The Seedbox germination kit consists of a tray with 12 containers and a transparent lid. It is like a small miniature greenhouse, the perfect environment for germinating seeds! The Seedbox also includes a Seedbooster bottle, a solution that will give your seedlings the right boost. Moisten the tray with water and Seedbooster. Wait about five minutes to give time to absorb the solution. Insert the seeds into the holes and place the lid on the tray. Transfer everything to a room at 20-24°C and in 1-5 days your seeds will germinate.

Other methods

In addition to germinating cannabis seeds directly into the substrate, there are other less reliable methods.

WET PAPER TOWEL METHOD

The first technique in our list of the least reliable germination methods is the popular "paper napkin method". This involves placing the seeds between a couple of sheets of absorbent, damp paper and closing them between two plates (or in any other suitable container, such as a dish rack). In this way, you will avoid exposing the seeds to light and can store them in a warm, dark place. Check the pieces of absorbent paper from time to time. If they dry, moisten them with a splash of water. Within a few days, your seeds should germinate.

The reason why we do not recommend this method is that the seeds should be touched and moved from the paper towel to their first pot immediately after germination. For young roots, these movements can have serious consequences (as the roots tend to anchor themselves to the paper), irreparably damaging the seeds. In addition, paper can become excessively soaked in water, causing the seeds to drown and rot.

GLASS OF WATER

Another very popular method of germination is to put the seeds in a glass of water. It seems a practical and simple technique: drop a few seeds in the water and wait for the roots to come out.

As with the paper napkin, the main problem with the water glass method is that it is not absolutely necessary. Between excessive exposure to water and the handling required in transplanting, your seeds run the risk of drowning or being damaged again. That said, some growers use this method to get a better idea of the vitality of their seeds. But if you are sure of the quality of your seeds and have turned to a reliable seedbank, there is no reason to go down this road.

ROCCIA WOOL

Stone wool germination is, in principle, a good way to start seed development, although it involves some more difficulties than other methods. Place your seeds in stone wool cubes, moisten them and place them in a tray or mini greenhouse. Wait a few days and your seeds will germinate.

Unlike other methods, stone wool protects young seedlings and allows you to transplant them safely into larger pots. However, rockwool must be soaked in water with a low pH before it can receive the seeds. Also, stone wool cubes tend to dry very quickly, which is why we only recommend this method to experienced growers.

TORBA (JIFFY)

The germination in peat (or jiffy discs) is an extremely valid method to start the development of the seeds. These token-shaped discs are moistened and, in a few seconds, they dilate and become larger and softer. The peat of which they are made is held together by an insoluble net. Make a small hole in the surface and plant the seeds.

After our preferred method of germination (sowing directly into the substrate), peat jiffy is definitely our second choice when planting seeds.

The flaw with jiffy is that the net that holds the substrate together does not always dissolve once transferred into a larger pot. In these cases, the net can trap the roots of the plants and hinder their growth. For this reason, we advise you to remove the net before transplanting, but be very careful not to damage the roots of the plants.

COFFEE FILTER

Germination with coffee filters basically follows the same principle as the paper napkin method. Place the seeds between two or more coffee filters, moisten them and place them in a bag or container (which you must then close).

As with the napkin method, we strongly advise against this useless and complicated technique. The risk of rotting the seeds or damaging them with tweezers during transplanting is too high.

Transplanting germinated cannabis seeds

If you adopt our preferred method of germination (directly into the substrate), sooner or later you will have to transplant your seedlings.

This will promote healthy plant growth, facilitate irrigation and fertilisation, and improve final yields. If a seedling has grown too long and is too fragile to be transplanted as it is, you can cover the stem base with more soil to support and stabilise the plant in the new pot.

To learn more about transplanting seedlings, see our blog When and How to Transplant Cannabis Plants to Increase Yields

Now that you know how to germinate your seeds, you can move on to the planting stage and all the subsequent stages.

CHAPTER 10 – Cannabis planting

So-called seedlings are small, new born cannabis plants. Once the cannabis seeds open, the main root, called taproot, pops out. After being transferred into soil or any other substrate, a young seedling grows until it emerges from the surface.

In their seedling phase, all cannabis varieties look the same and it is not possible to differentiate them according to their appearance. In order for the seeds to open correctly during germination they must be subjected to high humidity conditions. Once the taproot has sufficiently elongated, the first set of tear-shaped leaves will appear, supported by a thin stem. As it grows, the seed envelope will peel off on its own, but sometimes 'surgical' intervention may be necessary. These small leaves, called "cotyledons", begin to grow on top of the seedlings to function as solar panels, transforming light into energy.

Later, two more small leaves begin to emerge from the centre, with an appearance that already resembles a typical cannabis leaf. The seedling phase is quite short and it takes about a week or two before the young seedlings become real plants, although small in size. Technically, the seedling phase is part of the vegetative phase, but is often considered a separate development stage due to its particular requirements.

In fact, seedlings need more attention due to their small size and fragility. In this delicate phase errors can be very dangerous for the growth of the future plant. Here are some tips and tricks to give your seedlings all the attention they need.

THE MOST SUITABLE VASES

Once opened, the seeds are ready to be planted. The pot size for the seedlings should be relatively small. Simple disposable plastic cups can be used. Once they have emerged from the surface of the ground and grown for about a week, the seedlings can be decanted into larger containers. When new born seedlings are left in small pots for longer periods, the roots begin to grow around the sides of the pot and become tangled (a phenomenon known as root bound). This situation must be avoided, as the roots will no longer be able to absorb nutrients properly and the water may not be drained properly.

It should be considered that seedlings develop a surprisingly long taproot and by giving enough space for its growth you will allow the plants to stabilise and become stronger. The pot must be equipped with a solid drainage system. This can be done by drilling holes in the bottom of the plastic pots or simply by purchasing a container that already has holes in the bottom. In this way the taproot can dig and reach the depths of the substrate. Outdoors, the seedlings must be protected against pests.

You could possibly cut and peel off the bottom of a plastic bottle, drill a few holes and place it on the plant. This will allow sunlight to penetrate freely, airflow to circulate inside and your seedlings to avoid potential enemies. Many growers prefer to place photoperiodic seedlings directly into the pot, where they will complete their flowering. This minimises the stress created by the shock of transplanting. It is up to the grower to decide, as good results can be achieved in both cases. One thing is certain, auto-flowering varieties should never be transplanted, but grown in a single pot until the last day of their flowering phase.

SUBSTRATE FOR CANNABIS SEEDLINGS

The quality of a substrate plays a very important role. Clayey soils should always be avoided because of their ability to retain large amounts of water, excessive for seedlings and potentially dangerous. However, when a seedling is decanted into a substrate that barely retains water it can dry out. It is always best to choose a soil with a more open and soft texture, dark in colour and rich in nutrients, which is able to retain water without becoming too muddy after watering.

It is essential not to use soil treated with large amounts of fertilizer, often called 'hot soil'. Otherwise the nutrients will become toxic to the seeds. Although many pre-fertilized crop substrates work very well for seedlings, their fertilizer content should be minimal.

IRRIGATE THE SEEDLINGS

The seedlings must be subjected to a very humid environment to grow properly. During the first 1-2 weeks, the soil around the stem and taproot should be moist and wet. However, it should not be soaked, otherwise the seedlings will suffer. Try to think of it this way: when the soil looks soaked it means that it has been excessively wet, while if it moves easily away from the walls of the pot and is crumbly to the touch it is too dry.

If the pot should be larger than required by the plantula, then water it slowly, directly next to the stem so that the water descends gently along the entire taproot. Obviously, you will need to check the pH of the water, which should be within the 6.0-6.5 range. Do not wet the leaves of the seedlings directly, as the droplets could act as magnifying glasses, causing thermal damage and sunburn.

CANNABIS SEEDLINGS AND LIGHT

When young seedlings are grown directly outdoors, they can be placed directly under the sun without any problem. However, indoor growers may face some challenges. When young plants are placed under powerful lamps they can be under great stress and show more stunted growth. If the lights are placed too far away, the seedlings will tend to stretch out in an attempt to get as close as possible to the light source. In the latter case the plants will develop longer and thinner branches. This can also happen when the soil surface is too deep inside the pot.

Some indoor growers prefer to place seedlings under CFL bulbs because they do not generate too much heat. Normal LED lights or HPS lamps work well for this phase, as long as the seedlings receive less intense light than they will during the vegetative phase. Plantlets are like children: they cannot handle the amount normally consumed by an adult.

The heat emitted by the lamps can be excessive. The ideal temperature for seedlings is about 20-25°C. 18 hours of light and 6 hours of darkness will be fine. When young seedlings receive little light, they lose colour and become weak. If they receive too much light, they can overheat and run the risk of burning, a phenomenon called "light saturation". This means that the plants are receiving more energy than they really need to grow properly.

CHAPTER 11 - Determining the sex of Marijuana plants

Determining the sex of a Cannabis plant is the first step to get the best results.

One of the main skills you will need to develop is to determine the sex of a plant. There are male and female plants, and in some cases even hermaphrodite plants. The latter are usually female specimens that express the traits of both sexes.

When under great stress, female plants can develop male flowers and become hermaphrodite.

Cannabis plants are dioecious, i.e. they develop the male or female reproductive organs. Female plants develop the flowers from which the buds form, while male plants produce pollen. However, this plant species can behave abnormally. In certain situations, female plants can become hermaphrodite, which means that only one plant can develop both male and female reproductive organs. This happens under conditions of high stress, when the plant fears for its survival. In these cases, both organs are formed, which, by self-pollinating, produce the seeds, thus safeguarding the offspring.

From regular Cannabis seeds there is about a 50% chance that male plants will develop and another 50% female plants. The latter produce the much-loved marijuana buds, while the male plants develop flowers that release pollen. The male leaves can also produce small amounts of trichomes containing THC, but unless you are doing a particular scientific experiment, avoid wasting time with these plants.

Of course, beginner growers may not recognise the differences between the various seeds sold on the market. That is why it is so important to buy seeds from professional companies or specialist shops. In the early stages of development, it is impossible to recognise the sex of a Cannabis plant.

The only risk you might run when planting a regular seed is that a male or female plant will develop if the environmental conditions are good.

Identify the sex of a cannabis plant

Cannabis is a plant with similar characteristics to many other plant species, i.e. female plants have the ability to evolve by developing even male flowers. This is normally due to high environmental stress. In these cases, plants develop some male flowers at some point in their growth cycle, in order to produce seeds before they die from external causes.

The effort the female plant has to make to develop male reproductive organs is enormous. This phenomenon can be caused by a sudden change in light hours during flowering, a sudden change in temperature, drought and physical damage.

There are many other environmental factors that can cause a plant to change sex. An insect attack, an infection generated by a disease or the misuse of pesticides and fungicides.

This trend, however, is also a sign of genetic instability. A first quality, stabilized female Cannabis plant will hardly show signs of hermaphroditism when subjected to these types of stress. Of course, all marijuana varieties can develop both reproductive organs on the same plant.

Just as in the human kingdom, hermaphrodite plants are considered 'strange' beings and, in the case of cannabis, are even feared. Breeders and growers always suggest eliminating hermaphrodite plants from crops. The reason? They could accidentally pollinate the tops of female plants. If the hermaphrodite specimens were to release large amounts of pollen, they could fertilise the flowers of the other plants, preventing the formation of buds in favour of seed production.

WHEN THE CANNABIS PLANTS EXPRESS SEX?

The first sketch of the flower appears in the V-shaped corner between the leaf stem and the main stem of the plant. The so-called pre-flower comes out in the form of a microscopic light green ball. It normally develops during the vegetative growth phase. The same applies to clones.

There are two main ways to check whether the plants have become hermaphrodite. The first is to check the type of flower they have developed, the second is a test to be carried out at the end of the cycle. It is of course advisable to check for male flowers in the early stages of flowering. If, on the other hand, you find seeds in the buds of mature plants it means that some hermaphrodite specimens were present in the crop.

WHAT TO LOOK FOR

What any experienced grower would recommend is to buy feminized seeds from a reliable source.

However, as this is a problem that can occur in any crop, here are some tips to keep your plants under control.

Once the flowering phase has started, the female plants take a few more days to express their sex. Long white hairs, the pistils, come out of the pre-flowers. As they grow, the calyx and the structure forms which will then shape the actual top. The pistils of the female flowers are always white (never green).

The male plants, on the other hand, develop real "balls" which, once mature, will release the pollen. They normally appear one or two weeks after the beginning of the flowering phase. During the development they take the form of small yellow-green banana helmets.

When they have the possibility to ripen, the masculine flowers open releasing the pollen which will fecundate the possible female plants cultivated in the immediate vicinity.

Hermaphrodite plants develop both female and male flowers. This is why it is so important to remove them.

Although it may seem complex, it is a very simple manoeuvre to do. Growers who start a crop using top quality seeds and who maintain a good growing environment will have no problems. However, it is always advisable to observe the plants closely during their growth.

The differences between a male and a female flower are immediately apparent. We advise growers, even beginners, to grow more plants, to observe their differences, hone their growing skills and achieve increasingly rewarding results with each crop. From feminized seeds there is a 99% chance that only female plants will develop, but if someone turns into a hermaphrodite, simply remove them from the crop.

How to know if a female plant has been pollinated

A pollinated female cannabis plant will begin to produce seeds and devote less energy to producing quality buds.

It is always necessary to identify the male plants and the first warning signs of a possible pollination, promptly removing this threat to save the remaining females. In the same way, recognising a pollinated female plant in advance allows you to start again before it is too late, rather than continue with a crop that will result in a poor-quality harvest.

Among the first signs expressed by a pollinated female plant is the enlargement of the flower bracts, small leaf-shaped structures that protect the reproductive parts of the females. These are the sites from which the actual inflorescences develop, not to be confused with the calyxes.

A valid test to check if the bracts have swollen is to remove one with a pair of tweezers and open it. If there is a seed inside then the plant has been pollinated.

Another indication of possible pollination is the colour of the pistils. When a female plant is pollinated, the hairs that were previously white retract, becoming darker.

How to avoid pollination of female plants

Pollination requires the presence of male or intersex plants (hermaphrodite, i.e. female plants that also produce pollen). The first thing you need to do to minimise the risk of pollination is to remove as many male or hermaphrodite plants as possible.

Especially during the first three weeks of flowering it will be important to check frequently for the appearance of any male specimens within the crop.

Normally, a cannabis grower has no reason to keep the males alive and they will be eradicated as soon as they are identified. However, a breeder may be interested in growing both male and female plants, although he will try to separate them to avoid any accidental pollination. Normally, males grow in one environment and females in another. When grown outdoors, as in a garden, the males are often isolated in the most remote corner of the growing area, as far away as possible from the females. However, outdoors there will always be a risk of accidental pollination, as one gust of wind will be enough to carry the pollen.

How to recognize a male plant

To determine the sex of a cannabis plant you have to wait until the pre-flowering phase, when the plants begin to channel energy into reproduction. Female cannabis plants show their sex a few days later than males. In the areas where the inflorescences will develop (i.e. the nodes between stem and lateral branching), the first tufts of white hairs appear.

The male plants will never develop small hairs at the height of these nodes, but pollen bags, with the appearance of small balls. They may appear alone or in groups, depending on how advanced the pre-flowering phase of the plant will be. When the stage of development is advanced, the bags open by spreading their pollen in the surrounding areas and pollinating any female plants.

How to avoid pollination

Obviously, there is a way to avoid any risk of pollination in a domestic crop. Thanks to the innovation of the modern cannabis industry, feminized seeds are widely available in a wide selection of legendary new varieties. Unlike regular seeds, which have to be monitored to identify or separate males during growth, feminized seeds produced by the best seedbanks will only ever develop plants with exquisite inflorescences. Once this possibility has been assessed, it is up to you to decide which variety best suits your cultivation parameters and your personal goals as a grower.

CHAPTER 12 - Pistils Importance

A pistil is a female reproductive organ of the cannabis plant. For a normal domestic grower, the pistil is the 'hair' that protrudes from the calyx of a female flower. They can also be called stigmas. When a pistil comes into contact with the pollen of a male plant, the flower is pollinated.

In this case, instead of concentrating all its energy on producing more resinous flowers, the female plant starts to develop seeds. The cannabis will then become less potent and seeds will be formed in the bracts containing the egg. The "sensimilla", i.e. seedless marijuana, can only be produced if the female cannabis plants are not pollinated.

Pistils can tell you a lot about your cannabis plants.

Typically, in a marijuana crop, male cannabis plants develop pre-flowers before their female counterparts. After 3-6 weeks after germination you should be able to tell whether your feminized and photoperiodic seeds are really female, even though they are still going through the vegetative phase. Likewise, if you use regular seeds, you should be able to identify which male plants to remove before flowering.

Pistils tend to protrude from the nodes of young cannabis plants quite randomly. Inspect your cannabis plants carefully and, sooner or later, you will see the pre-flowers appear during their vegetative growth. Sometimes they are more evident near the apical parts of the plants and quite easy to spot. But this is not always the case, so observe your plants very carefully.

The pre-flowers are visible next to the stipules (those little green hairs that grow on the stem at the nodes). Growers always hope to see large tufts of white hairs coming out of the knots. If you see small balls and no whitish hairs then the plant is male. However, until you can see the white pistils coming out of the knots you can never be sure you have a female cannabis plant.

Some cannabis varieties can take up to 8 weeks of vegetative growth before confirming sex. However, after 4-6 weeks, the sex of the male plants will be evident and can be eradicated. And if necessary, keep an eye on those two or three uncertain plants that may have already started flowering.

Auto flowering cannabis plants tend to suddenly explode and flower much faster than you might expect. At some point between the 15th and 35th day after germination, the feminized seeds of auto flowering cannabis varieties will already show white pistils from the first flowers in development. After about a week, the buds will begin to form swollen, glistening goblets of resin. The pistils will quickly change colour from white to orange/red in a matter of days, not weeks.

With photoperiodic cannabis varieties, flowering can be divided into three sub-phases: beginning of flowering, intermediate flowering phase and end of flowering. Pistils are a perfect indicator for evaluating the stage of development of female cannabis plants. During the first weeks with 12/12 light cycle the pistils keep a bright white colour. However, between the 4th and 6th week (mid-flowering), the first orange, red and/or pink colours will begin to appear and gradually spread throughout the plant. But only between the 7th and 10th week, after a good washing of the roots with water alone or with a solution specially formulated to eliminate fertilizer residues, most pistils will have taken on a beautiful red, orange and brown shade.

Which Plants have Pistils?

Only female plants and intersex (or hermaphrodite) plants develop pistils. Unfortunately, intersex plants also produce pollen and are a great threat to female plants, as they behave like male plants disguised as females. In addition, stress can also lead a cannabis plant to develop intersex traits. Some industrial hemp varieties are specifically hybridized because of their hermaphrodite characteristics.

Do you want to get a good sensimilla? Make sure that every pistil in your female plant is not pollinated. This means that you will need to continue to monitor your plants during flowering. An interrupted or disturbed cycle of darkness is perhaps the main cause of stress from which hermaphroditism results.

Before the advent of microscopes and zoom lenses, growers had to rely only on their intuition when harvesting cannabis. Good old visual control of cannabis flowers is a reliable and proven pre-harvest practice. Most cannabis growers harvest when 75% or more of the pistils have taken on darker colours. The flowers covered with red, orange, pink and brown hairs are now ripe.

Even without advanced optical systems, you can see the gleam of trichomes. Also, the buds will be sticky to the touch, but avoid touching them too much (unless you plan to do a little charas). Also, the pungent aromas released by the ripe buds should be a clear signal that your female plant is now ready to be cut. As you can see, all five senses play an important role. Pistils are a valuable visual aid throughout the entire cannabis life cycle.

CHAPTER 13 – Trichomes in Cannabis

The word trichoma comes from the Greek "Tríchōma", which means "growth of hair". Since they are microscopic, you have to zoom in on the crystalline resin mantle that covers every high-quality cannabis bud in order to see the trichomes, which look like many stems with small mushroom-shaped heads.

It is thought that in nature trichomes promote certain survival functions essential to the cannabis plant. The sticky resin coat is a primary defence against fungi, insects and herbivorous predators.

Some flies and fungi are unable to penetrate the trichome barrier, while terpenes eliminate the smell of lettuce, discouraging any hungry hairy creature.

In addition, trichomes could play a key role in allowing cannabis to grow in adverse weather conditions. The resin layer gives the wild grass protection against violent winds, from desert sirocco to Siberian blizzard.

Trichomes even act as a natural barrier against the sun, protecting marijuana plants from the effects of UV rays.

Trichomes are small factories dedicated to the production of cannabinoids and terpenes. Power, taste and smell are inextricably linked to the process in the cells of the small mushroom-shaped heads.

Cannabinoids include compounds such as THC and CBD, which provide marijuana with its mental and physical effects respectively. Terpenes are "unsaturated hydrocarbons", or aromatic hydrocarbons, which provide the buds of different species with different tastes and smells.

Trichomes are microscopic super-structures, which encapsulate the essence of the psychoactive properties of cannabis. They can also help the grower decide the optimal time to harvest the herb.

By checking the colour variation of the resin-filled ends with a camera or microscope, the grower can best assess the ripeness of the flowering female marijuana plants. From the beginning of flowering until about halfway through the phase, the resin heads will be transparent in colour.

During the final phase of the flowering cycle, the grower will notice the transformation of the small mushroom heads from transparent to milk-coloured and finally amber.

Experienced growers will see the mix of milk and amber as the precise time to harvest. Of course, many other factors are important to assess the maturity of the flowers, but we advise you to let the trichomes guide you to avoid harvesting too early or too late. Check those little white heads.

The relationship between trichomes and light is essential to understand the immense importance of trichomes. Ultraviolet light is what gives the best quality grass the X-factor.

Cannabis plants feed on light, and when they receive the optimal light spectrum, they offer better performance. The anecdotes told by old school outdoor growers, that grass grown indoors under high lighting levels (HID -high lighting levels) sometimes lacks aroma and potency, have been confirmed by modern science.

Trichomes respond positively to UV rays, and it is now thought that UV rays are needed by trichomes to produce certain types of terpenes and cannabinoids.

Modern LED lighting systems seem to bridge this gap, being specially designed to emit the optimal light spectrum for cannabis plants, more efficiently than high illumination lights.

FUN THINGS TO DO WITH TRICHOMES

We have therefore confirmed that a nice resin coat is responsible for the best qualities of cannabis.

Trichomes are the foundation of all kinds of concentrated and wonderfully potent hashish.

The method of extraction can vary from the Moroccan method of sifting the plants and subsequent pressing, to the hashish oil produced with butane gas, which can be transformed into "budder" at low temperature. The basic material is always trichomes, and they can be easily separated from the rest of the plant.

Sometimes this can happen too easily and accidentally, so remember to always handle the buds very carefully, because resin-filled heads break easily and dried buds can deteriorate quickly if stored inappropriately. Concentrates have the big advantage of unlimited shelf life.

Trichomes are not the only parts that make up cannabis, but they are certainly the most important. The spread of dabbing among smokers in the new millennium and the international legalization of CBD medical products confirm that trichomes are increasingly important in cannabis culture.

The Green Revolution is no longer exclusively linked to smoking sticky weed. The knowledge of trichomes opens the door to culinary cannabis recipes, fantastic concentrates, tinctures, and a variety of medicines and extraordinary new options yet to be discovered.

However, some of the best advice and cultivation techniques are purely anecdotal.

One hypothesis suggests that cold weather could expose plants to a beneficial form of stress. It is also believed that lower temperatures prevent volatile terpenes from degrading during the last days/weeks of flowering. We cannot therefore guarantee that this technique will work, but it is still worth a try.

INCREASE TRICHOMES PRODUCTION

Among cannabis growers there are some rather unusual tricks to increase trichome production, such as washing the roots with ice water, which would increase the amount of trichomes, terpenes and cannabinoids. This makes ice water an inexpensive and simple way to increase the potency and flavour of crops.

The root washing is done around the last week of the flowering phase. Growers water the plants with large amounts of water to remove nutrient build-up and, consequently, to improve the taste of the buds. There is no scientific evidence to support increased trichome production due to washing the roots with ice water.

CHAPTER 14 – Cloning Cannabis plants

Cloning means getting a perfect copy of a Cannabis plant by taking a portion of a branch ("cutting") from a mother plant. The cutting is then stimulated to develop its own root system, thanks to which it will grow into a plant that is almost identical ('clone') to the mother plant. Cloning is a simple, quick and cheap way to get new cannabis plants.

The special thing about cannabis cloning is that each clone will have the same genetics as the mother plant. This means that the new specimens that will develop will have qualities and characteristics identical to their parent. Cuttings taken from a female plant will all show the female sex. If you have in your hands a variety of Cannabis with special qualities, with, for example, delicious flavours, high potency or high productivity, you can get dozens of copies of this plant for free.

How to get clones from your Marijuana plants

Cloning Cannabis involves cutting a portion of a branch of a plant, stimulating it to develop a new root system. However, by doing a quick search on the internet on how to clone Cannabis, we find that there are conflicting opinions on the best way to get cuttings. However, although cloning techniques may change, there are some guidelines that apply to all cases. In order to start a cloning process as correctly as possible, you must first select the best and healthiest plants from which to take cuttings. Let's take a closer look at the main steps to follow in order to clone Cannabis.

What you need to do to clone a cannabis plant

- A healthy "mother" plant from which to take cuttings
- A scalpel, a razor blade or sharp scissors
- Substrate cubes (cubes of stone wool and special substrates for cloning, such as Rapid Rooters)
- Rooting hormones in gel or powder
- A light of "slight" intensity for the development of clones. You can use low power CFL bulbs or, even better, special lights for clones.
- High-grade alcohol for instrument disinfection

- Optional: Heating mat, mini-greenhouse or similar solutions, "low pH" product

How to pick up clones

First of all, we need to assess whether the Cannabis plant is ready to be cloned. To recognise the stage of development that lends itself best to this process, wait for some side branches of different sizes to develop. Look for the portions that have not developed from the same branch, as is the case with younger plants.

Once you have selected the plant to clone, you will need to clean and disinfect all the tools you use. Know that freshly cut clones are very sensitive to bacteria, microorganisms and contaminants. It is therefore essential to clean the tools and the work surface.

Read carefully the instructions for the substrate cubes you have chosen to root your cuttings. Soak the cubes in water for several minutes before use. Stone wool cubes normally have a rather high pH. For this reason, it is recommended to leave them soaked in water until the pH is lowered to 4-4.5.

Take a cutting. The best place to cut a portion of the plant is on a new, well-developed branch. Cut about 10-20cm from the tip of the branch, making a 45-degree angle cut. You are free to take any portion of the plant. You can cut off any branch, but the lower parts of mother plants tend to develop roots faster than the higher parts. This is why lower branches are better suited for cloning.

As soon as you have cut the Cannabis clone, soak the lower part in a glass of water. This helps to prevent air bubbles from forming inside the stem.

If there are leaves in the vicinity of the cut and in the internodes above, cut them too. Large leaves require a lot of energy produced by photosynthesis, to the detriment of the energy to be used for the formation of new roots.

Although some growers are able to obtain clones simply by using water, there are products based on rooting hormones that can encourage cuttings to develop new roots in a much shorter time. Rooting hormones are available in gel or powder form. Simply immerse the cut from the bottom of the cuttings in the gel or powder to isolate them from the surrounding air. Some people use both products, first dipping the cuttings into the gel and then into the rooting powder. Always read the instructions for your products so that you know how to use them as correctly as possible. Always try to cover uniformly the whole area of the cut that you are going to insert into the substrate cube.

Carefully place the clone inside the groove of the cube. You should apply light pressure to the bottom of the cube so that the groove around the stem of the cuttings is slightly closed.

If you have an automatic cloner, mini-greenhouse or similar solutions, use them to protect and improve clone growth. These accessories maintain a high moisture content inside. Young clones have not yet developed roots and therefore need to absorb large amounts of water from the surrounding air. Although not indispensable, mini greenhouses and kits to maintain high humidity can help when cloning.

Monster cropping cloning technique

Taking cuttings from a flowering plant is not recommended for beginners. However, if you have some experience in marijuana cloning, Monster Cropping is a technique that is always worth trying. It consists of taking cuttings from a 30-day flowering plant.

The steps to follow are the same as described above.

Monster Cropping is a rather apt term for this type of technique. The clones you get are not normal cuttings, but real monsters. Once they have taken root, the new plants will begin to grow, showing an extremely vigorous growth and developing a multitude of very thick and strong lateral branches. Initially, the leaves will look deformed and the branches will start to grow chaotically. From these cuttings you will not develop perhaps the most beautiful plants you have ever seen, but the harvests you get are loaded with numerous buds.

How to grow new clones

Clones must grow under optimal conditions, with high temperatures and high humidity. If you do not have a mini-greenhouse, spray water on the clones several times a day. Try to maintain a humidity level above 70-80%. The ideal temperature for clone growth is slightly above the ambient temperature, 22-25 ˚C. If outside conditions are colder, you can use a heating mat to keep the temperature under control. Some commercially available cloning kits have small integrated heaters with adjustable temperature.

Clones do not require light during the first two days. After a couple of days of darkness, place them under a CFL bulb or special lights for growing clones and seedlings, so that they can grow healthy and exuberant. If you want to use the lighting system you usually use for growing, you may need to move it away so that the light intensity is reduced. The important thing is not to provide clones with 24 hours of light per day, but instead to maintain a cycle of 18 hours of light and 6 hours of darkness. The roots tend to grow more in the dark phase.

Clones will be ready to be transplanted when the roots begin to emerge from rockwool or substrate cubes.

ADVICES

Remember that clones have not yet developed roots and need high humidity conditions. Spray water several times a day on their leaves to keep them moist, especially the first week. Watch out for mould. If the clones are protected under a mini greenhouse, open it several times a day, so as to air the inside and prevent the formation of mould.

It is not essential, but you can add a very light nutrient solution in the water to be sprayed, so as to further stimulate the growth of the clones.

Make sure that no contaminants enter the gel or root powder. Even the smallest particle could ruin all your cloning efforts in a short time. Do not directly immerse the clones in the gel or root powder container. Pour the amount you are going to use into a separate container and store the original in a cool, dark place. In this way you will immerse the cuttings only in the small amount of root hormones necessary for cloning.

When you clone a Cannabis plant, the reproduced plant will have the same age and growth stage as the mother plant. One of the best times to take cuttings is a few days before the mother plant blooms.

Do not hesitate to take more clones than you really need. Not all clones will survive, especially if you have little experience in this field. It is always better to root more clones, considering possible losses.

Be patient. Most clones should start rooting after a few days, but some may take several weeks before showing the roots.

You can keep the mother plants from which you take clones for long periods of time in the vegetative phase. Prevent them from starting their flowering phase by keeping them under light cycles of 18 hours and 6 hours of darkness. Under these conditions, mother plants can produce ramifications from which new cuttings can be taken for several years.

CHAPTER 15 - Seeds vs. Clones

The cultivation of cannabis plants is a source of countless pleasures. Growing them requires care and patience, and a casual interest can easily become a real passion. If you are thinking of starting a cultivation for the first time, you have taken the first step on the road to becoming a true marijuana connoisseur.

As a beginner grower, you must make a fundamental decision before embarking on your new adventure. Do you intend to grow your plants from seeds or using clones? You may not yet be aware that there are two ways to grow cannabis plants, each of which has its pros and cons. Choosing the right option can make the difference between success and failure. The information below should help you make the right choice.

n clone is a tip of a branch cut from a mature cannabis plant, which can be replanted and grown to produce buds. Growing a plant from a clone that has already partially developed may seem like a simple task, but in reality, it can be much more difficult than growing a seed from scratch. First and foremost, all plants are highly susceptible to diseases such as fungi or insect infections. A clone represents the exact genetic image of the mother plant from which it comes, so if the mother suffered from any health problems, the cut branch will also suffer. If you are a novice grower, you may not have the experience or knowledge to deal with these problems, and the plant may die.

The only tangible benefit of using the cloning method for a new grower is that the plant is already farther along in development than a seed would be, and you can hope for an actual yield sooner. If time is not an issue, this may not matter to you at all. It usually only shortens the entire growing cycle by about a month. In addition, most people find that they really enjoying the experience of learning to raise a cannabis plant from its earliest stages. It's a bit like experiencing a birth, and you can be proud of your adult plant once it flowers knowing that you grew it from seed on your own.

The condition of the clone may pose other obstacles. A freshly cut clone needs a lot of loving care, and when it is replanted for the first time it will be extremely sensitive. An initial shock period is expected after sowing, and very specific amounts of light and nutrients will be needed to overcome this phase. Sowing failure is all too common, and a new grower may have to fight to keep young clones healthy.

Another major problem with the use of clones is the difficulty of tracing them. You will need access to a mature mother plant and, of course, permission to cut off a branch. In such circumstances, how can you guarantee the variety of cannabis that will be produced? Will it be of good quality? This will remain a mystery until you are ready to try it. Some clones can be purchased online, but this is an extremely risky way to buy plants. For clones the transport can be traumatic, and you risk receiving a clone in very poor condition. Sometimes plants on the market are treated with pesticides or fungicides, and a clone from these plants will contain these elements.

The only tangible benefit of using clones for a new grower is that the plant develops faster than it does with a seed, and a faster actual harvest can be hoped for. If you don't have time problems this may not be of interest to you, as it usually shortens the whole growth cycle by about a month. Also, most people really appreciate being able to learn how to grow a cannabis plant from an early stage. It's a bit like having the experience of a birth, and you can be proud of your adult plant when it blooms, as you will know that

you have cured it seed after seed on your own.

Choose seeds for cultivation

Probably starting to grow new plants using seeds is a guaranteed and easier method for inexperienced growers. If growing a plant from a tiny seed sounds like something scary, you can rest assured that in reality this method is much less difficult than when using clones.

Firstly, there are big seed banks like Royal Queen Seeds, which offers a tested and authentic product that you can rely on, in fact there can be no doubt about seeds from a seed bank. If you can control the variety you buy, you know well in advance which variety of cannabis you will get, which means you won't waste time with a poor-quality plant. Royal Queen Seeds also offers feminized cannabis seeds, which give rise exclusively to female plants, and since only female plants produce buds, you can be sure that your money won't go to waste on plants you can't use.

Another reason why the method of growing seeds is considered optimal is that it is the most natural method for the cannabis plant itself. Marijuana is, in fact, an annual plant, which means that its life in its natural environment lasts about a year. Marijuana plants are therefore not genetically designed to stay active and flower for longer periods of time, so a clone from a mature plant can already become old, and generate fewer buds than a seedling.

If you think that clones will produce buds faster than a seedling, consider the fact that Royal Queen Seeds offers auto flowering seed varieties. Autoflowering seeds have been carefully crossed and air conditioned in an area of the world with long hours of sunlight. This means that these seeds have been exposed to lighter than they need to flower, over a period of 2 to 4 weeks.

Finally, a plant grown through seeds will have a strong root system. For those totally inexperienced in gardening, a taproot is the central part of a plant's entire root system, which extends deep into the surrounding soil and absorbs large amounts of nutrients. A clone is unable to grow a taproot and can never be as strong and healthy as a plant grown from seed, which will develop its taproot instead.

Although the clone growing method has once gained in popularity, growers concerned about the individual quality of their plants are returning to the seed growing method. A look at the wide range of top-quality seeds available online can convince you that the method using seeds is the best way to succeed as a grower.

CHAPTER 16 - Marijuana Pruning

Cannabis plants that grow naturally, without being bent or pruned, can offer exceptional yields. However, this is only true for two particular growing environments: the first is a private, large, open-air garden with sufficient warmth and natural light; the second is an indoor SOG of at least 1m² in area.

In the first case pruning or folding is not necessary due to the natural path of the sun. As the earth orbits around the sun, the light angle received from outdoor cultivated plants moves continuously. Therefore, all parts of the plant will receive a sufficient amount of sunlight at some point during the day.

The second case can be applied to any indoor growing space when a grower decides to use the SOG, or Sea of Green technique. This technique requires a large number of cannabis plants grown in tightly packed square pots/containers to optimise the whole growing area. In this case a short vegetative phase is set, to harvest as soon as possible and limit the overall height of the plants.

Clones tend to be more effective, but Indica varieties that are more stable and uniform or autoflowering varieties can work just as well from seed. Again, there is no need to prune the plants. Each specimen of cannabis grown with SOG technique normally produces a large, single, elongated central bud, and a few side branches.

Pruning Techniques

All growers, regardless of their experience, can experience pruning. The following pruning techniques will increase your yields if you can apply them correctly.

CIMING

Topping is the simplest pruning technique for doubling the tops. It simply consists of removing or pinching the apical top or main branch. Be sure to apply this technique only during the vegetative growth phase, preferably when the plants have reached a height of 30cm.

The two buds below the cut will develop into two new apical buds. Also, after topping the cannabis plants redistribute their hormones in all branches, encouraging them to grow more vigorously. This technique gives the marijuana a bushier structure and can be repeated several times to take up all the growing space.

The only drawback of topping is that the plants take a minimum of one week to recover from shock, thus prolonging the vegetative growth period. This period can be further extended if you decide to prune the plants several times or even prune the more developed side branches. We would also like to remind you that topping is not suitable for autoflowering varieties, because these are plants that come into bloom too quickly.

THINNING OUT THE LOWEST BRANCHES

Among the simplest pruning techniques suitable even for beginner growers is thinning the less developed and lower branches of the plants. It is always best to cut down the lower branches during the vegetative phase, but remember to prune them sensibly without removing too many branches and leaves.

The first sets of branch pairs can be removed and reused. Why not try cloning them? After 3-4 weeks of vegetative growth it is always advisable to cut the two sets of lower branch pairs to increase airflow.

This thinning allows the cannabis plants to concentrate all their energy in the apical parts closest to the light, from which the buds will develop. In addition, the lower branches are also the oldest and tend to be easier to root during the cloning process. Do not throw them away. Combine thinning with cloning to make it easier to rotate your crops.

Excessive thinning can stress your plants, making their growth more stunted or forcing them to become hermaphrodite. So, try not to exaggerate. Time is also essential in thinning. Early pruning when the plants are still young can cause some problems, but cutting the lower branches during flowering can also be counterproductive.

Thinning to increase yields and avoid any risk must be carried out between the third and fourth week of vegetative growth. This technique can also be applied to fourth generation auto-flowering varieties.

FIM

FIM or "Fuck I Missed" is a variation of the accidentally discovered topping (hence its name). To apply a fimming, simply remove 75% of the apical end of the top or tip of the main branch. As with topping, the grower can use scissors or finger tips. Most growers prefer to pinch the apical parts, as the main objective here is not to make a clean cut.

The pleasant reward for this technique is that the plants develop 4 or more apical branches instead of the 2 normally obtained from total topping. Again, fimming is not recommended for auto-flowering varieties.

LOLLIPOPPING

Lollipopping is another pruning technique to increase yields whose results tend to be better when the branches are pinched between the fingers rather than cut with scissors. The big difference of this technique is that you have to wait until the flowering phase before cutting. Applying lollipopping on a cannabis plant at the third or fourth week of flowering results in branching with lollipop-shaped buds.

Removing all the lower buds and leaving only the taller ones from which the larger buds will develop allows the plants to take on a heavier structure. The branches will look like long green lollipops. As in the case of the 3 previous techniques, it is always recommended to combine lollipopping with the ScrOG technique.

In fact, it would be a crime not to exploit the potential of lollipopping by amplifying it with a Screen of Green. By channelling all the energy of the plants towards the apical parts and avoiding wasting light to illuminate the lower, less productive and more leafy flowers, lollipopping also improves the quality and quantity of the final product. There will be fewer leaves but the flowers will become larger. Also, instead of having to think about how to reuse manicure waste and popcorn inflorescences, you will only end up with a good supply of first-class marijuana.

CHAPTER 17 - How to Set the Lights

Contemporary indoor growing usually uses at least one of these 3 artificial light sources: HID, CFL and LED. Growers often use a combination of grow lights. Of course, there are other types of older lighting technology but they are all quite outdated. This blog will focus on the lights used by growers in the 21st century. We will go into the practical side of the cultivation room tips in depth without dwelling on pseudo-scientific information.

HID or high-intensity discharge lamps have been the choice of every type of indoor grower, from beginners to professional growers, since at least the early 90s. Over the years, lamps have become more efficient and ballasts have become digital and reflectors improved and bigger. Growers who prefer HIDs believe that lumens are the only yield statistics that matter when it comes to lights.

Sure, CMHs or ceramic metal-halide have arrived on the scene and the 315W bulb is impressive but it is an expensive upgrade for a standard MH or metal-halide. Plus, the 315W CMH doesn't perform as well as a dual spectrum/agro HPS 600W or, a high-pressure sodium lamp. CFLs, similarly, show some promise but are far from the tested and reliable HIDs.

LEDs or light emitting diodes are the emerging technology that seems to end the reign of HIDs for cannabis cultivation. The latest generation LED systems are capable of producing marijuana of a quality comparable, and in some cases superior, to a classic HID system. PAR or synthetically active photo-active radiation is the measure that is considered most important by LED users.

HID

Although HIDs have had some slight improvements lately, the basic principle of cannabis cultivation with this type of artificial light remains the same. MH for vegetative growth and HPS for flowering. Although dual spectrum HPS lamps are a popular alternative and probably better for autoflowering genetics.

The 400W and 600W bulbs are best suited for indoor cannabis growing. The lights should be hung level. The optimal height of the lights or OLH is between 30-50cm above the tops of the plants. This means that you have to carefully tie the reflector to the ceiling or the top of the grow box with pulleys or ropes.

It is best to use hanging objects that can be easily adjusted and repositioned during plant growth. However, seedlings and clones may suffer from the intensity of a 600W MH lamp, a distance of 60cm upwards may be more appropriate during their growth stage.

Do not mess with light rails unless you have engineering credentials. Steady lights that don't dance, horizontal level bulb contained in a clean, open reflector is standard for professional growers. Ideally, you should use a large reflector or, large enough to cover your growing space, a wide aperture to take advantage of the whole area.

Air-cooled glass filters, lights and lamps are expensive. What's more, cool tubes are only suitable for closet cultivations, as they have the worst reflective properties compared to any other existing reflector. Adding more lights and more fans would mean higher electricity bills.

LIGHTING AND GROWING SPACE

Typically, 400-600W per m² is enough for domestic cultivation. Commercial growers could push over 1000W for maximum yield. Placing as many lamps as possible in the cultivation is not a solution for a big harvest. More HID lamps mean more light but also more heat. These lamps produce heat. 250W lamps are only for small growers.

The only advantage 250W lamps offer is that the plant buds can stay close to the bulb up to 20cm. The heat output is much lower than 600W but, the light will not penetrate deeply. If the light is limited, it will not reach the low branches of tall plants.

The addition of a single 600W HPS lamp can massively increase the temperature of the growing area. Often, a less expensive and more efficient solution is to invest and upgrade the grow room. Maybe coat the walls of Mylar or change from a magnetic ballast to an adjustable digital ballast or change strategy to LED lights.

The answer is many or few, depending on the grower's preference. You can put 16 cannabis plants in square SOG containers within a 1m² space. Alternatively, a grower can fill the same space with a large plant using the ScrOG method. In both methods, the yield will be similar. Again, it is all about how the light is used and the growing area.

CFL

CFL lamps, also called compact fluorescent lights, are truly efficient in the cold and white spectrum as an alternative to MH bulbs. A 250W CFL lamp can give results comparable to a 400W MH lamp. This can be achieved by hanging the CFL as close as 10cm from the top of the plants. CFLs are cold lamps and can be brought close to plants without burning the leaves. In addition, CFL lights increase the cultivation temperature marginally. This makes them perfect for seedlings, clones and for use during the vegetative phase. CFL lights are sometimes the only option for micro cropping.

Unfortunately, CFLs do not have powerful lumens and PAR spectrum. Also, the worst thing is that they are not effective for flowering marijuana plants. Cannabis plants need more intense illumination than a CFL can offer during the flowering period. Expect small yields and uncompact buds if you use CFLs during the flowering phase.

LED

The latest LED systems have finally reached parity with traditional HID lighting systems. At the moment, the situation is similar to when the first flat screen televisions became available. The benefits and disadvantages were clear to everyone. However, the limiting factor was the high and prohibitive prices imposed by the major companies.

High output LED kits that consume 350-400W and can make like a 600W MH or HPS with a full spectrum are not cheap. There are some models that are. The best LED systems, they can operate producing little heat and are incredibly economical in the long term. The distances from the tops of the plants vary differently, so those who use them should pay attention to the instructions provided by the manufacturer.

Below we will go into the science behind the light output so that you can evaluate the wattage and position of the lamps for growing cannabis. We will deal with terms such as photons, lumens and PAR, as well as the main types of lights for cultivation and their differences.

Light spectrum

Light is made of photons, tiny particles that travel inexorably at the speed of light. The photons of light rays vibrate at different frequencies and wavelengths. The human being can see photonic radiation in a wavelength range between 380 and 680nm, while the sensitivity of plants to light ranges from 200 to 800nm. Not all wavelengths within this spectrum produce the same effects on photosynthesis. Those that most activate biochemical processes in plants are called PAR (photosynthetically active radiation), with a spectral range between 400 and 700nm.

Light can be measured in photometric quantities, derived from the sensitivity of the human eye to colour, or in radiometric quantities, correlated instead to the energy transported by light rays. Lumen and lux are the photometric units commonly used to indicate the light perceived by the human eye.

However, photometric measurements do not indicate the amount of light energy that a lamp sends to a plant to activate its photosynthesis, as they do not include PAR variables. Nevertheless, lumens and lux can still give an initial indication of the light output of a given lamp and can be used to compare different products by measuring their photometric efficiency through the lumen: watt ratio (regardless of any differences in the light spectrum output at different wavelengths).

Lux and lumen are appropriate units of measurement for evaluating the power of MH, HPS, CFL and T5 lights, but they are not suitable for accurately measuring the efficiency of an LED light during cannabis cultivation.

Watt calculation

In principle, the minimum amount of broad-spectrum light required for a cannabis plant is about 9,000lm/m², while the optimal amount is over 20,000lm/m². However, in indoor crops, the growth and flowering of a healthy, strong plant depends on the light thresholds reached at specific wavelengths, which are sufficient to trigger photosynthesis. That is why LED grow lights use radiometric systems to measure the number of irradiated photons in the PAR colour frequencies mentioned above.

The most widely used radiometric measurement in horticulture is PPFD (photosynthetic photonic flux density), a parameter that indicates the flow of photonic PAR micromoles per second in one square meter ($\mu mol/m^2/s$).

Assuming that the cultivation light provides the PPFD, we can calculate its radiometric efficiency and compare different lighting systems using the PPFD ratio: watts.

Sun, lamps and correct photonic pressure

The midday sun in the middle of summer reaches the earth at latitudes of about 45°, with a photosynthetic power from 1,200 to 2,000 PPFD. However, cannabis seedlings, clones and mother plants are already happy with a PPFD of just 200-400µmol/m²/s. In the vegetative phase, however, adult plants require 400-600µmol/m²/s, while in the flowering phase 600 to 1,500µmol/m²/s of PPFD, with the normal atmospheric levels of CO_2. A study found that the best PPFD to push cannabis plants' productivity to the limit ranges from 1,500 to 2,000µmol/m²/s, with temperatures of 25-30°C and normal CO_2 levels raised to 750ppm.

Although cannabis is a rather demanding plant, irradiation above the threshold for each variety, stage of development or environmental condition does not necessarily increase yields. On the contrary, excessive photonic pressure can cause damage to leaves and flowers. In other words, the production of buds increases when the cannabis plant receives 20 to 30 moles of PAR light per day, and then stabilizes at between 30 and 40 moles.

Lighting your grow room?

To determine the correct amount of light for a cannabis crop you have to multiply the length of the grow room by its width. This will allow you to calculate the growth area, which you will then have to multiply by the desired PPFD level.

If your grow room should be 250cm wide and 80cm deep, the growing space will be 2.50m x 0.80m = 2m². If you are aiming to have flowering plant canopies with a width of about 2 square metres and want to experiment with a PPFD level of 500µmol, you will simply need 1,000µmol/m²/s. To ascertain the required power, this result will have to be divided by the PPFD per watt of light.

Rule of watts per m2: how many plants can you grow?

LED lighting systems produce a higher PAR than MH, HPS and other lamps. Nevertheless, your plants will need the same number of watts per square meter to produce a similar yield as traditional HID lamps. It should also be noted that LED lighting systems are often advertised with a higher than actual electrical power, but this does not mean that a 400W LED can cover the same square meters as a 1,000W HPS lamp. Here are some general graphs of the power needed to grow healthy and vigorous cannabis plants using different lighting systems. During the early stages of vegetative growth, they will need about half the power.

As a point of reference, HPS lights can cover approximately the following areas (relative to plant crown width):

- 250W ≈ 0.5-1m² ≈ 2 plants
- 400W ≈ 1-1.5m² ≈ 4 plants
- 600W ≈ 1.3-2m² ≈ 8 plants
- 1000W ≈ 1.8-3m² ≈ 10 plants

LED lights cover the following areas:

- 120W ≈ 0.5m² ≈ 1 plant
- 200W ≈ 0.8m² ≈ 2 plants
- 280W ≈ 1m² ≈ 4 plants
- 350W ≈ 1.5m² ≈ 6-8 plants

To get an idea of how much light intensity you are giving your plants, get a lux meter and measure the light intensity at different points in the canopy. Alternatively, you can make a theoretical calculation that considers the lumens emitted by the lamp in relation to the growth area. To calculate the lux pressure on the canopy, simply divide the lumens of the lamp by the square metres of the illuminated surface. If you place a lamp that produces 100,000lm at a distance of 1m from the apical parts of the plants, it will illuminate a surface of 1m² with an intensity of 100,000lx (100,000lx ÷ 1m = 100,000lx). If the lamp is only 0.5m away, then the apical parts of the plants will receive 100,000lm ÷ 0.5m = 200,000lx.

Unfortunately, the light intensity decreases by a factor equal to the square of the distance of the source from the illuminated object. This means that the same lamp positioned at two meters will increase the width of its beam, covering 4m², but with only 25.000lx. In this case, you will need four lamps to reach your hypothetical 100,000lx target over the entire cultivation area.

Rules for the right distance

HID (MH, HPS)

HID lamps are available in two versions: metal halide (MH) with cold light more suitable for the vegetative phase, and high-pressure sodium (HPS) with a much wider spectrum for the flowering phase. These lamps generate a lot of heat and require an adequate cooling and air extraction system. They also emit less light over time. This means that a new bulb should be placed at a greater distance than an old bulb and then replaced after a couple of years of use.

The most appropriate distance for MH and HPS lamps depends mainly on their wattage. Always start by positioning the light at the upper end of the range and gradually lower it. Assuming the ventilation system in the grow room is set up correctly, with a 250W lamp you can start at a distance of 35cm and gradually descend towards the foliage until you reach 25cm from the buds in the last weeks of flowering. With a 600W lamp, however, you can start at 50cm and descend to 30cm. If you use a 1000W lamp, you should keep a distance of at least 80cm.

A very common practice is to keep the back of your hand facing the light, just above the apical parts of the plants. If you feel comfortable, so will your plants. But don't trust the general rules too much. Always check your plants for signs of overheating or excessive photonic pressure.

LED

LED lighting systems generate much less heat than HID lamps, but still need a cooling source to prevent accidental burning of plants. LED lights emit a large amount of light pressure, even at relatively low temperatures. This amount of light, and not the heat, can cause burning and leaf whitening.

Depending on the model, the optimal distances between LEDs and plants may vary, but manufacturers are used to include the appropriate information inside the packaging. Start with the average distance of the recommended range and observe how the plants react in the following days. Turn off the lights if you notice that the leaves are turning pale or showing burnt tips. If the plants are happy, bring the LED panel closer, but never so close that the taller leaves bleach, turn yellow or burn.

High power LED panels over 300W must be kept at least 70cm away from the canopy and then brought closer during the flowering phase. As a landmark, 200 to 400W LED lights should be positioned between 30 and 70cm away from the plants, while 450 to 600W lights require a distance of 50-80cm. The most powerful lighting systems should be positioned at an even higher height. Remember to keep an eye on the plants every time you start using a new lamp.

CHAPTER 18 – Types of Lighting for Cannabis plants

The intensity of light emitted by a lamp is one of the essential factors in growing healthy plants and producing powerful buds.

Although natural sunlight provides optimum light intensity for Cannabis cultivation, many growers prefer to grow indoors for a number of good reasons. Firstly, not everyone lives in climate zones suitable for outdoor Cannabis cultivation. In addition, the artificial lighting of an indoor grow, regulated with special timers, allows for much better control of all the necessary parameters during the vegetative growth and flowering phase of the plants.

Today, different models of lamps for indoor cultivation can be found on the market. However, not all lighting systems are the same. There can be huge differences when it comes to efficiency and cost. Let's take a look at the various light models available on the market and try to highlight the pros and cons.

Fluorescent Lamps for Growing (CFL)

CFL stands for "Compact Fluorescent Lights". These bulbs are easily purchased in many stores, including household goods stores, but also more general stores. These lamps lend themselves very well to small indoor crops, making initial investment rather low.

Pros:

Their availability and affordable prices outline the main advantages of CFL lamps. These lamps require a standard socket, which allows them to be used with any luminaire. The most commonly used fluorescent lamps in Cannabis cultivation range from 40W and up. They are available in different colour temperatures: 'daylight' from 6500k or 'warm white' with a redder light spectrum of 2700k. Fluorescent bulbs with a "daylight" spectrum are better suited for the vegetative growth phase, while "warmer" bulbs are better suited for the flowering phase, for the redder light they emit.

Against: - the "hotter" ones are more suitable for the vegetative growth phase, while the "warmer" ones are more suitable for the flowering phase, for the redder light they emit:

The light intensity of CFL bulbs is lower than other grow lamps. To provide sufficient light, they must be placed very close to the plants. If you are not planning to install a large number of CFL fluorescent bulbs, CFL bulbs are normally better suited for small indoor crops with only one or two plants. However, daylight CFLs are ideal for illuminating clones and seedlings in their early stages of growth.

As mentioned above, CFL lights are not as efficient and powerful as other lamp models. However, for those approaching the magical world of cannabis cultivation for the first time, they are an excellent starting point.

Hid lamps for growing (MH & HPS)

HID (High-intensity Discharge) lamps for cultivation have now become the standard adopted by all major Cannabis companies. Many growers are convinced that HID lighting systems offer the best results and the most abundant yields.

There are two types of HID bulbs, MH (Metal Halide) and HPS (High-Pressure Sodium). The difference between the two lights is that MH emits a "cooler" and bluish light, while HPS emits a redder light spectrum. This means that MH bulbs are more suitable for the vegetative growth phase, while HPS bulbs are more suitable for the flowering phase.

Most experienced growers use lighting systems where they alternate MH and HPS lamps depending on the growth phase the plants are going through. If you are forced to choose only one type of HID lamp, for use throughout the life cycle of your plants, rely on an HPS from the start.

The 600W HPS are the most commonly used HID lamps for growing, as they offer a good balance between light intensity and electricity consumption.

Growers interested in growing with HID lamps can find complete sets including lamp, ballast and reflector on the market.

Pros:

HID lamps are still quite cheap compared to other lighting systems for growing. They are easy to install and use and have proven over the years to offer a standardized and reliable solution with which to achieve excellent results.

Cons:

The power of HID lamps from 600W and upwards emits a great deal of heat. This means that they must be flanked by suitable inlet and outlet ventilation systems to properly oxygenate and cool the entire Grow Room. In addition, HID lamps tend to lose light intensity over time. Their life span is rather limited. In an indoor cultivation it is always recommended to replace them with a certain frequency. Some growers prefer to replace them once a year, others use them a few months longer.

Also, HID lamps cannot simply be plugged into a normal electrical outlet, but need a special power supply to turn on properly. This high energy demand is reflected in a significant increase in electricity bills.

LED grow lights

Until a few years ago, LED lights were not recommended for 'seriously' growing Cannabis. They were only suitable for growing seedlings and cuttings in their early stages of growth.

However, LED technology has come a long way in recent years.

Modern LED grow lights emit more lumens per watt and the latest COB ("Chips on Board") technology now provides a light intensity adapted to the plants' needs, with increased light penetration. Today, LED lights can compete with or even outperform other models of cultivation lamps, including HID lamps. However, they must be chosen with extreme caution to find the best plants specifically designed for Cannabis cultivation.

Pros:

LED lights are the best grow lamps in terms of energy efficiency, requiring low power consumption. This means that they can meet the lumen demand of the plants without increasing running costs. Another advantage of LED light is that they emit much less heat than HID lamps, without almost increasing the indoor temperatures of an indoor cultivation. This will allow for much less heat problems and the plants will not run the risk of being 'burned' by the excessively high temperatures in a Grow Room. In addition, unlike HID lamps, LED lights do not require separate power supplies for proper operation, as they are powered from a normal power outlet.

Against: the opposite:

Compared to other lighting systems, the initial cost of purchasing LED lights for cultivation may be quite high. These are high-end LED devices with the most modern lighting modules, with prices that could easily scare. On the other hand, if you plan to grow them with a certain frequency, the lower running costs of LED lights and their low heat emission could quickly pay off the initial investment.

It is still worth noting that, unlike HID and CFL lamps, the LED market does not guarantee standardisation of its products. This is why the market has been flooded with poor quality LED grow lights, poorly designed lighting fixtures and sold with false and outrageous claims. When it comes to LED lights, you have to prepare for a significant initial investment. That's why we recommend that you do your research and always rely on a reliable, albeit expensive, brand.

But then what is the best lighting system for growing cannabis? It depends on many factors, including the size of your growing area, the running costs you are planning to incur, and last but not least, how much you can and are willing to spend.

If your indoor growing requires high light intensity, you will need to consider installing powerful lighting systems during the flowering phase to achieve the best yields (such as 600W HID lamps or equivalent LED lights). However, if you are more interested in growing one or two plants, or simply want to light some cuttings or seedlings, then you can use much less powerful lamps.

CHAPTER 19 - How to Make the Most of LED Lights

Before you buy an LED for cultivation, you need to know the various models available today. There are currently three main types of LED lights that can be used to grow cannabis, each of which has its pros and cons. The choice of LED model to use will depend on what exactly you are looking for and how much money you are willing to spend.

STANDARD LEDS ("PURPLE")

These standard models were the first LED lighting systems made available to growers and are still widely available today. These lamps are equipped with dozens, sometimes hundreds, of small to medium power LED lights (3 to 5 watts per LED) distributed on a compact device. Sometimes cannabis growers refer to these lamps as 'purple lights' because they often include a combination of red and blue LEDs, which together emit a shade of purple light.

The biggest advantage of these standard models of LED lights is their price. Most of them are produced abroad and you can easily find them on eBay or other online shops. However, their disadvantage is that they are often not of great quality. They tend to be less reliable and their light intensity is often lower than other LED models, which also leads to lower yields. To overcome this disadvantage, lately standard LED lights with COB LED or UV LED technology in addition to red and blue are in circulation. This seems to improve the yields and the quality of the tops.

COB LED

COB stands for "chip on board." A COB LED consists of several hundred tiny LEDs directly integrated on a single small chip, unlike the LEDs of different colours distributed over the entire surface of the device (as in the previous case). COBs are among the most efficient LEDs on the market. They emit a very intense white light that comes very close to the natural light spectrum of the sun. One advantage of COBs is that they provide excellent light penetration into the plant canopy due to their intensity, thus allowing final yields comparable to those produced by quality HID lamps. Their light spectrum is also optimal for the growth of healthy, strong plants and they are much more energy efficient. The only drawback could be that a high-end COB LED lamp can cost much more than the cheaper 'purple lights'.

Some grow lamp manufacturers combine several COB LED lights into one luminaire, often equipped with lenses and reflectors. There are also other models with only one COB, which can be a good alternative for larger growing areas, as they can be arranged evenly to better distribute light over the whole area. Most growers use COB LEDs with a light spectrum that works for both the vegetative and flowering phases, but you can also find those with the spectrum ('colour temperature') specially calibrated for the vegetative or flowering phase.

SPREAD-STYLE" LED

Spread-style" LED lights consist of a large number of small LEDs distributed on a large panel or plate. Spider-style and rack-style LED lights, widely used in commercial greenhouses, also belong to this family. Spider-style LEDs do not use flat panels, but "arms" as spider legs equipped with LEDs. The main advantage of spread-style LED lights is that they are among the most energy efficient LEDs, which means you can get the maximum light intensity for the wattage used. One disadvantage is that high-end spread-

style LEDs, such as spider-style lamps, can be extremely expensive.

The advantages of growing with led lights

We have already said that LED lights have several advantages over other lighting systems for growing cannabis, such as HID lamps. Here is a complete overview of why you might want to opt for LEDs in your next growing operation.

1. LED LIGHTS ARE MORE ENERGY EFFICIENT

Compared to HID lights, LEDs are much more energy efficient. They consume less electricity and in the long run reduce bills considerably. Although high-end LED lights can be quite expensive, the investment is almost always worth it because the savings will pay off the higher initial costs over time. Similarly, high quality LED luminaires will last even longer than HID lamps, whose performance tends to decline over time, requiring frequent replacement. Good LED light can last for several years without requiring any maintenance.

2. WORK BY EMITTING VERY LITTLE HEAT

LEDs generate much less heat than HID lights, which can be a great advantage as you don't have to install additional cooling systems in your grow room or closet to maintain optimal temperatures. This is particularly advantageous if you grow in summer or live in warmer climate zones. The downside is that if you live in a cold region you may need to use a heater in the colder months. But because LEDs save money over time, the potential running costs of a heater are easily recouped.

3. WITH LEDS, PLANTS CAN GROW MUCH CLOSER TO LIGHT

LEDs produce less heat, which means that they create less stress on plants, which can be brought closer to the lights without negative effects. Higher light intensity translates into higher yields!

4. LED LIGHTS REDUCE THE IRRIGATION PROGRAM

By emitting much less heat, the potting soil will remain moist longer and the frequency with which you will have to irrigate will decrease. If you have just switched from HID lamps to LEDs and are used to seeing your plants thirsty all the time, you will need to be very careful with your watering programs under the LEDs, otherwise your plants may receive excessive amounts of water.

5. CONCIMATE LESS

When watering cannabis plants, you normally do so with an infusion of water and fertilizer. So, as well as requiring less water, your plants will also need less nutrients than their previous needs. So, in addition to the obvious savings on fertiliser, the less frequent irrigation and fertilisation programme will also reduce the risk of salt build-up and, consequently, of nutrient blockages and nutrient deficiencies.

Grow with led

As we mentioned earlier, many types of LEDs emit a fixed light spectrum that works for both the vegetative (growth) and flowering phases. In this way you can use the same lamp for the entire plant development from sowing to harvest.

Although many consider this to be the most practical option, some growers prefer to fine-tune their LED lamps to achieve the best results and optimise their light efficiency at every stage of growth. To this end, some commercially available LED lights have a switch to activate a light spectrum for the vegetative or flowering phase. Here are some other factors to consider in each growth phase.

A) LED LIGHTS AND SEEDLINGS

As soon as the seeds have sprouted, your future cannabis seedlings will need light to grow. However, compared to adult plants, seedlings are much more sensitive to too much light. For this reason, you need to be careful when starting their growth with powerful LED lights.

If the light intensity of your LED lamp can be lowered, do so. If you cannot, move the lamps higher away from the seedlings. However, make sure you do not raise them too high, otherwise you risk the plants growing too narrow and tapered.

Likewise, if your LED has a switch to activate a spectrum for the vegetative or flowering phase, set it to the vegetative phase, which normally emits a 'cooler' bluish light, ideal for this early stage of development. Set the timer to 18 hours of light per day and 6 hours of darkness.

As the seedlings become taller, stronger and ready for the vegetative growth phase, gradually increase the light intensity.

B) LED LIGHTS DURING THE VEGETATIVE PHASE

Set the lighting to 18 hours of light per day and 6 hours of darkness. Some growers prefer light cycles of 20-24 hours a day to maximise vegetative growth.

Always monitor the development of your plants. If all goes well, they should grow strong, healthy and lush. If they should grow tapered and lanky, then they are most likely not getting enough light. Increase the intensity by lowering the lamps towards the canopy or using the light switch, if your lamp model has one.

How long your plants will grow in the vegetative phase will normally depend on how much space you have available. Technically, you could grow your plants under 18-24 hours of light for as long as you want, but there will come a time when you have to spend them in bloom, otherwise they will become too big. Know that some cannabis varieties can grow considerably longer (doubling or tripling in height) during the first weeks of flowering. Take this into account when deciding when to set the timer for the flowering phase.

C) LED LIGHTS FOR THE FLOWERING PHASE

Photoperiodic cannabis starts flowering in late summer, when the days begin to shorten naturally. In indoor crops the grower will have to force flowering by setting the light program to 12 hours of light and 12 hours of total darkness. If your LED light has a flowering switch, use it.

When plants flower indoors under a 12-12 light cycle, it is very important that the 12 hours of darkness are never interrupted. So, make sure that no light from outside enters your closet or greenhouse. This could cause the flowering plants to resume vegetative growth or cause other problems such as hermaphroditism.

If your LED has a switch to modulate the intensity, it is time to turn the light on at maximum or lower the lamp on the plants to the recommended distance for the flowering phase. If you are not sure of the distances, almost all grow lamp manufacturers make the appropriate recommendations available.

Important: If you change something in the lighting, for example if you increase the intensity and/or lower their position, be sure to do so gradually, over a few days, rather than doing it all at once. A change that is too sudden can put too much stress on the plants.

If you are growing auto flowering instead of photoperiodic varieties, you don't have to worry about switching to 12 hours of light on/off to start flowering. You can leave your autoflowering plants at 18-24 hours of light per day until harvest. And even then, if your LED light is equipped with a flowering switch, you will need to use it as soon as your autoflowering plants start flowering. This will help to increase yields.

Which lights make the tops grow better

Are there any differences between the quality of the ropes and the yields obtained with LEDs compared to those with MH HID lamps? Some growers claim that MHs produce better yields and 'nicer buds' than LEDs. But there are also those who say that although HID can give more abundant yields, with LEDs you get buds that taste better and/or have better overall quality. Of course, what is really "better" remains open for interpretation.

For more information on the differences between LEDs and other cultivation lighting systems, you can also read our article on the pros and cons of different models of cannabis grow lamps.

ADVICES

Modern LED lights, such as COB lights, can emit light as bright as HID. If your plants are too close to LEDs, you could cause "light burns" with discoloured and bleached leaves, nutritional deficiencies and all sorts of growth problems. For this reason, it is very important to keep LEDs away from cannabis plants.

There is no distance recommendation that works for all types of LED lights, as they vary greatly from model to model. It depends on the amount of light emitted by your LED, whether or not there are lenses and reflectors, and so on. The manufacturer of your lamps should advise you on the best distances from the canopy, referring them both to the instructions provided in the package and on his website. As a general rule, however, most LEDs are kept at a distance of about 30-45cm from the tops of plants to ensure healthy and vigorous growth.

CHAPTER 20 - Dark Cycle

When cannabis plants, like other green plants, are in an illuminated environment (whether sunlight or artificial) they perform photosynthesis. This is the method by which they convert light into energy and release oxygen. They also breathe. In contrast to the misinformation that circulates everywhere, plants breathe continuously, just as all aerobic organisms do. They stop when they die and they die if they stop. Cannabis plants only produce a surplus of oxygen during the day.

During the dark cycle the cannabis plants do not carry out photosynthesis and continue to breathe at a constant rate. They do not only breathe when there is light. Calvin's cycle, which is independent of light, processes all solar energy into carbohydrates. The roots also breathe and it is therefore very important that they grow in a well-ventilated substrate. Take advantage of air pots to keep your substrate oxygen rich.

Photoperiod cannabis is sensitive to changes in the daylight it receives. In fact, photoperiod cannabis varieties cannot go from vegetative growth to flowering without a long period of darkness. 12 or more hours of darkness biologically trigger flowering in photoperiod cannabis plants. Outdoors, when the nights gradually begin to stretch (from the summer solstice onwards), some varieties can start flowering when they receive 14 hours of sunlight.

Only auto flowering seeds have a predetermined post-germination life cycle. It is believed that the auto flowering characteristic is an adaptation to the 24 hours of continuous sunlight that occurs in Siberia. Authentic autoflowering varieties begin to flower after about 30 days of vegetative growth.

VEGETATIVE GROWTH: 18-6 OR 24-0?

Photoperiod cannabis varieties can be kept in vegetative growth indefinitely until they receive 14 hours or more light per day. The debate is about what is the optimal light-dark ratio for a growing cannabis plant. That said, most indoor growers agree on an interval between 18 and 24 hours a day. Outdoor growers start in spring/summer to take advantage of the longer days.

The 24-0 light cycle could speed up vegetative growth. The downside is the electricity bill. Cycle 18-6 is the most common because it equates to long summer days and is slightly cheaper. The only substantial difference we have discovered with our experiments is that cuttings exposed to a light-dark cycle of 18-6 give better results than those under a 24-0 cycle.

Today the new alternative of vegetative growth with the 6-2 lighting program is also in fashion. Applying these three light-dark cycles within 24 hours means that the cannabis plant receives the same amount of 18 hours of light and 6 hours of darkness as a conventional 18-6 cycle. In addition, this is a feasible option as photoperiod cannabis plants need 12 hours of continuous darkness to flower. Just think that these short intervals of 2 hours of darkness give the plant a chance to rest and process the CO_2 more effectively. In addition, 6-2 avoids light saturation and is the potentially most effective light-dark cycle for photosynthesis.

THE STANDARD INDOOR CULTIVATION PROCEDURE

12-12 is the equitable division of 12 hours of light and 12 hours of darkness and occurs naturally only near the equator. Indoor growers rely on artificial timers configured with this light-dark cycle. During the day or period with lights on, the two red phytochrome receptors and the red-distant phytochrome are balanced. In the dark, the red-far-away becomes red. It is the increase in red colour that triggers the flowering. Many growers leave the plants in complete darkness for 36 hours before starting cycle 12-12 to ensure a high red phytochrome ratio.

However, even if you grow a seed photoperiod variety with table 12-12, it will take 3 to 4 weeks before the buds start to form. Photoperiod cannabis is an annual plant. Marijuana can survive with just 8 hours of light per day and photoperiod plants that are in bloom can return to the vegetative phase. The vegetative phase will start again with the restoration of long days.

Sunlight interruptions occur in the form of clouds. Cannabis plants can handle them. Any period of pitch darkness, without light pollution, will be sufficient for photoperiod varieties. An infiltration of light into the growing area when the lights are off will stress the plants and disturb the flowering. This can stress a plant and make it become hermaphroditic. Street lights can confuse outdoor cannabis with photoperiod, preventing it from flowering. Only bulbs with green light can be used if you have to intervene or enter the garden during the dark cycle.

Grow boxes and growing rooms should be checked for holes or tears. Greenhouses can be covered to ensure that the night phase is completely dark for as long as necessary. It doesn't take long to plug a hole or buy a light-proof tarp. Instead, breaking the dark cycle during flowering can cost you the loss of an entire harvest.

If you want high power and maximum yield, we recommend a light-dark cycle of 18-6 or 20-4. However, if you keep the lights indoors at 24-0, your plants and equipment such as fans will also be pushed to the limit. So far, auto flower crops grown at 24-0 have not been able to outperform those with 4 to 6-hour dark cycles.

CHAPTER 21 - Feeding flowering plants

During vegetative growth, your cannabis plants will need high doses of N (nitrogen). When your plants move into the flowering phase, it is important to concentrate on fertilizing the flowers. If you continue to feed your flowering plants with nitrogen-rich fertilizers, they will grow more leaves and branches than flowers.

Flowering cannabis needs more P (phosphorus) and K (potassium) than N. As a result, the grower will need to change nutrients with the flowering nutrients. This can become a problematic change in the feed table and could make the pH of the water different from the solution for vegetative growth.

Too much N during advanced flowering will slow down the story. Flush with pure water or a light flush solution in the last 12 weeks of flowering will make a difference. Waiting for the pistils to turn 50% red/orange is a good time to start flushing. It is better to be patient instead of concentrating on overloading your plants with flowering boosters.

Let the flowers ripen, wait for the trichomes to peak production and finish by flushing. Use a microscope to observe the flowers towards the end of the eighth week for auto-flowering and indicate them. Check that the trichome heads are white and amber. It will probably be worth continuing the flush during the ninth week if your herb is not yet ripe. Early harvesting can leave you with a supply of immature buds that have not yet reached the peak of trichome production.

Coffee Dregs as Natural Fertilizer

Coffee grounds are easy to procure and can be of interest to different farmers, especially those who care about sustainability. Coffee grounds are completely vegan and, if you use your own coffee grounds or those from the local market, transport emissions are also minimized. You can also use organic coffee grounds if you are particularly concerned about pesticide use and aim to have a completely organic crop.

Coffee grounds could be used for your cannabis seedlings, both indoor and outdoor. Not only that, coffee grounds can also help to cover some obvious odours and protect plants from pests and other pests.

Here are the main reasons why using coffee grounds for your seedlings is a great idea.

INCREASES ACIDITY

Coffee grounds, as well as compost, increase the degree of acidity of the soil. Cannabis plants thrive in a slightly acidic environment, with optimal pH values around 6.0-6.5. A soil pH too high or too low will make plant growth difficult, so it is vital to monitor acidity closely. Coffee grounds can be used as an acidifier if the soil is too alkaline. In addition, being completely natural, they will not harm the environment at the time of subsequent disposal.

PART OF THE COMPOST

When the grounds are removed from the coffee machine, they can be added directly into the composter. The waste materials inside the composter have nutrients that keep your seedlings in good health. Unlike when they are put directly into the soil, when the grounds are added to the compost they become "green matter", which can then be mixed with the carbon-rich "brown matter" such as straw and wood ash.

Such a mix is excellent for generating the heat needed to decompose the rest of the materials into a quality compost.

Coffee grounds provide important amounts of nitrogen to the compost. This mineral is vital for plants because it is the main component of chlorophyll, the green pigment that plants use to carry out photosynthesis. Coffee grounds are a good source of nitrogen and help to avoid any possible harmful deficiencies during the whole life cycle.

SHIELD AGAINST PARASITES

Probably one of the most challenging aspects of cannabis cultivation is pest control and management. There are many creatures greedy for nutrients in the cannabis plant, and they can cause serious damage when they attack in groups. If taken in time, many infestations can be successfully resolved, although preventive measures are much more effective than curative ones. Coffee grounds offer several advantages when it comes to erecting a barrier against pests.

First, the acidity of the coffee prevents infestations. Secondly, the small, rough particles in the grounds have a micro-abrasive effect. This means that insects trying to get to the plant through the ground may be discouraged by the minefield created by the coffee.

In addition, the grounds also provide a shield against other small animals and fungal infestations, such as Fusarium, Pythium and Sclerotinia.

WORM FOOD

Worms are an important resource in many cannabis crops because they act as small composters. Vermiculture is the exploitation of this quality of worms. Their organic secretions are used as soil compost. Coffee can be food for the worms as long as they also have other organic material to eat, so as to avoid a diet that is too acidic.

DIY Cannabis Plant Fertilizer

Of course, making your own fertilizer can seem complicated. But it's not. Actually, it's very simple.

You will most likely find nitrogen, potassium and phosphorus in various leftovers and natural ingredients in your pantry or fridge.

To prepare nutrient-rich soil at home, you need to start with composting. Composting is an activity that is sometimes repellent to some growers. Some people think it is too complicated, smelly, chaotic and demanding. However, composting can be very simple to do.

In fact, you could start composting today. All you need is dry soil or dry pruning waste from a garden or yard (if you have it), and a compost bin (which costs about $80 on Amazon, but you can easily make it yourself).

When the bin is ready, you need to start adding dry material first, followed by wet material (bread crumbs, coffee grounds, tea or herbal tea, etc.).

The only real rule for good composting is this: keep your compost mix not too dry, and not too moist. Check your compost bin regularly, adding water (if too dry) or dry material (if too humid).

Over time, the microbes in the compost will decompose the ingredients you have put in and produce a rich, well-ventilated soil that is ideal for your plants. If you prefer, you can add earthworms for an even better result. Of course, this may be difficult to achieve if you have limited space or live in an apartment.

Your compost gets the nutrients from the ingredients you add in the bin. If you don't like the idea of composting, don't worry. You can add these ingredients directly into the soil where your plants are located (but remember that in this case they will be assimilated over a longer period of time).

You need to know which natural ingredients to use as natural fertilizers to get healthy and strong marijuana plants. Probably many of them are already present in your kitchen.

INGREDIENTS

COFFEE FUNDS

Coffee grounds are perfect for composting. They decompose easily and contain all 3 essential elements useful for growing lush plants. They are particularly rich in nitrogen, but also contain good amounts of potassium and phosphorus.

BANANA PEELS

Banana peels are rich in phosphorus and potassium. They also contain calcium and many other minerals that help enrich the soil and make the plants stronger.

AQUAFABA

Aquafaba (or "legume water") is the liquid found in cans of chickpeas, lentils, peas and other legumes. It is an excellent source of potassium (just like the beans/peas themselves). You can add this water directly into jars, or better still, use it to moisten the compost if it gets too dry.

COOKING WATER

Do you know the cooking water that remains in the pot after cooking spinach, cabbage and other vegetables? Next time, before washing the dishes, don't throw this liquid into the sink. Use it instead to feed your plants. When you boil vegetables, a lot of nutrients are dispersed in the water and can be easily absorbed by the plants.

The nutrients in the water vary depending on the vegetables you have cooked. Cooking water generally contains potassium, calcium, iron and other minerals. Always remember to let the water cool down before feeding it to the plants.

URINE

This point may sound a little disgusting. However, human urine is one of the best fertilizers for cannabis plants because it is rich in nitrogen.

If you decide to give your plants urine, remember to dilute it in water first. Avoid direct wetting of the foliage as the high nitrogen concentration can damage the leaves, stems, etc.

CITRUS PEELS

Like most fruit peels, citrus peels are an excellent natural fertilizer for plants. They are rich in nitrogen, potassium and phosphorus. They are therefore a perfect and complete fertilizer to be added to compost or directly into the soil of plants.

Citrus peels also keep pests away. They can therefore protect cannabis from mites and other harmful insects.

EGGSHELLS

Eggshells are full of calcium. Although calcium is not an essential element for plant nutrition, it does promote the proper development of cells.

Keep in mind that eggshells can take a long time to decompose. It is therefore better to put them in compost instead of adding them to the soil.

HERBES

Any combination of herbaceous plants is perfect as a fertilizer. Nettle, for example, is a rather annoying plant. If you touch it with your bare hands you may feel itchy all day long. But it can also be used to make tea, and to make a fertilizer. Nettle is rich in various nutrients.

For example, you can take some branches of nettle, symphite or mille-feuille, put them in a watertight container filled with water, and leave them to macerate for a couple of weeks or months.

CHAPTER 22 - When and how to harvest Marijuana

Knowing when it is time to harvest cannabis is essential if you want to get the most out of your plants. A simple oversight could ruin an entire harvest, producing lighter, less tasty buds. These mistakes are mainly made by beginners, and inexperience can often lead to mismanagement of the final stages of a plant's growth. To prevent you from making the same mistakes, you will need to follow what is described below.

Interpreting signals

When they are ready to be harvested, female cannabis plants send clear signals. The grower will need to sharpen their eyesight and control the behaviour of the plants during the last weeks of flowering. Falling and yellowing of the leaves are the first visual sign, as the cannabis plant is now going through its period of senescence.

In addition, the size and resin production of the buds cease to increase. The pistils curl up on themselves and dry out, showing predominantly orange/red and brown colours (although some still retain a certain turgidity and a whitish colour). Pay close attention to these signs in the last weeks of flowering.

INDOOR CANNABIS

Most photoperiodic cannabis varieties grown indoors are ready to be harvested after 8-12 weeks of flowering at 12/12 light cycle. Until the grower reduces the light cycle from 18/6 to 12/12, the plants maintain their vegetative growth indefinitely. Autoflowering cannabis varieties, on the other hand, can be harvested in just 8-10 weeks after germination, with a constant light cycle of 18/6.

OUTDOOR CANNABIS

If, on the other hand, you grow photoperiodic outdoor cannabis varieties, then the development phases of the plants will be dictated by Mother Nature. The seeds need to be planted in the right season to get the best results. The naturally decreasing hours of sunlight stimulate the plants to start flowering at a much more gradual pace. Starting in spring/early summer, growers know that the fruits of their labour should be ready in early autumn. Not to mention that in the

Emerald Triangle (Emerald Triangle, Northern California) October is also called "Croptober" (from "crop", harvested in English).

Sativa-dominant varieties may require a little more patience and normally flower in 3-4 months. Hybrids and Indica-dominant varieties are faster and generally ready to be harvested after 2-3 months of flowering. A photoperiodic outdoor cannabis crop requires several hours of work on the part of the grower. Basically, from the day you sow to when you can finally harvest the buds can take 6 to 9 months.

In recent years, autoflowering varieties have had enormous success among outdoor growers and beginners. These plants flower with age and not because of a variation in the hours of light they receive. They are more predictable growing varieties and are often the only option for those who live in colder climate regions with shorter summers. In addition, their autoflowering property allows outdoor growers to get even more harvests per year.

Observe trichomes closely

We strongly advise you to get a pocket microscope. The most precise method to assess whether cannabis is ready to be harvested is to observe the stage of development of the resin glands. The best time to cut it is when the spherical head of the trichoma, supported by its thin stem, has taken on a milky white colour. If you want to get the maximum potential from your buds, this is the best time to harvest.

When the trichomes are transparent it means that they are still immature and when they become amber it means that the THC is starting to degrade. Normally, Sativa-dominant varieties should be harvested when the trichome heads are partly milky white and partly transparent to get an extremely euphoric and stimulating 'high'. Indica varieties, on the other hand, can be harvested when the trichomes are partly milky and partly amber, with a slight predominance of amber. The higher the prevalence of amber, the more intense will be the sedative and "block-diverse" effects. Trichomes take on these more amber tones when THC is converted to CBN. Just like many other things in life, it all depends on taste.

Root washing before harvest

Regardless of the substrate, growing system or fertiliser you are used to use, all cannabis crops only reach their full potential when they undergo a good

120

root wash before harvest. When there are 2 or 1 weeks to harvest, stop fertilizing your plants and water them with plenty of water. You can use specially formulated flushing products or simply water with water.

The flavours of your marijuana will be much more enjoyable, as washing the roots during the last two to one week of flowering allows the accumulation of salts and fertiliser to escape from the substrate. When a proper root flush is not achieved the final product can have unpleasant and irritating flavours on the throat. Let the substrate dry for a day or two after washing and proceed with harvesting accordingly.

Harvesting kit

Scissors to clean the tops (sterile and preferably of a good brand)

Latex/Vinyl gloves (preferably vinyl)

Cardboard boxes perforated on the top to allow air to pass through during the drying of the tops. Paper bags for the bread where to dry the "popcorn" tops, the lower and less developed ones. Alternatively, a fishing line or a string stretched between the two sides of an empty cupboard can recreate the perfect drying environment.

Dehumidifier (an economical model is sufficient)

Thermometer/hygrometer (take the one in your grow cabinet)

A black trash bag (to put the waste parts, such as branches and large leaves)

A sheet of baking paper (with which to cover the table on which the tops will be cleaned)

A cane and music (the harvest takes time and 100g per hour is already a job well done)

Isopropyl alcohol (to remove resin residues on latex gloves and scissors. On vinyl gloves, on the other hand, the resin peels off more easily. Simply rub the scissors' blade on their surface to remove the sticky hash).

Sharp knife (very useful for scraping hash off gloves and/or scissors after harvesting).

How to harvest cannabis in 3 simple steps

1) CUT (SCROG FRIENDLY)

Do not cut the main stems at the base unless you are growing small Indica or autoflowering varieties. Domestic growers are used to applying different pruning and bending techniques to increase yields. For the best-known ones, such as topping, fimming, LST and ScrOG, it is always recommended to do it branch by branch. Cutting plants grown under a ScrOG net at the base is a bad idea. Instead, try to remove the side branches by cutting them close to the main stem.

2) MANICURE

The ideal is to cut the whole plant at the base or gradually cut all the branches leaving the stem anchored to the pot. However, professional growers always tend to harvest from top to bottom, especially when using the ScrOG technique or if the plants have been grown outdoors reaching monstrous dimensions. Take your pace and try to do a good job cleaning up the freshly harvested buds.

The larger resin-free leaves and branches are waste material, but can still be recycled for compost and/or infusions. Start cutting these parts and, once removed, move on to the sticky inflorescences. Handle the tops with care and as little as possible. Try to support them from the branch. Resin-covered leaves are a valuable material to make a good hash, so try to remove them carefully, avoiding damaging the underlying buds. Once cut, put them in a paper bag. When the small leaves surrounding the buds and branches without flowers are not removed, you can create optimal conditions for mould and fungus. In addition, the small leaves spoil the appearance and taste of the final product.

3. DRYING

The cannabis buds should be dried slowly in a dry, dark place, evenly and evenly for a period of 10-15 days. Sunlight degrades the THC. Larger buds should be placed in cardboard boxes, while medium and small buds should be placed in paper bags or on tight ropes inside a wardrobe. Check the tops every day and avoid touching them constantly. If you use shoe boxes, be sure to rotate the ropes every day to ensure even and accurate drying. In the same way, shake the paper bags with the smaller lines every two days. If you want to adopt a good alternative solution, try CVault's marijuana tanning containers. We recommend them!

Put your thermometer in the boxes and keep the optimal drying conditions constant: room temperature and 50% relative humidity, or at least try to stay close to these values. If necessary, put a dehumidifier in the cabinet.

Congratulations! You have just learned everything you need to know to harvest cannabis as correctly as possible.

MANICURE SCRAPS

Keep all those little crystal-covered leaves you cut near the tops. Put these scraps aside and dry them in brown paper bags, like the ones used for popcorn tops. Leave them to dry for a week or two, transfer them to an airtight Tupperware and put them in the freezer. This will save you time until you have decided what kind of concentrate to turn those crystal-covered leaves into. With resinous waste you can get magnificent pollen, BHO and Shatter.

CHAPTER 23 - How to Dry and Tanning Fresh Cannabis Peaks

The process of growing cannabis does not end at harvest time. Fresh marijuana needs to be dried and treated properly to prevent the formation of mould. These procedures also result in a tastier and more intense herb.

Difference between drying and tanning

Drying, as the name suggests, involves drying fresh buds so that they contain less moisture to be properly smoked or vaporized. On the other hand, tanning involves storing the buds in closed containers for a period of at least two weeks. This helps to develop the taste and aroma of your buds as they ripen.

Tanning is extremely important because it helps to preserve your grass so that it can be preserved over time while retaining its unique flavour and maximizing potency. When you harvest your buds, they contain excess sugar and starches that may be attacked by bacteria and enzymes in the air. So, by fertilizing your buds you encourage the degradation of these nutrients by making the final smoke smoother and better tasting.

Marijuana Trimming

There are two main methods for trimming the buds at harvest time. Wet trimming involves cleaning the buds immediately after harvesting. On the other hand, in dry trimming, cleaning of the buds takes place after drying and before tanning. Ideally, we recommend trimming while the buds are still wet, as it is easier, more precise and does not risk losing resin through agitation as when handling dry buds. That said, dry trimming can make a product exceptionally well cared for, worthy of a prominent position just for its appearance.

In order for your buds to dry evenly, we recommend that you make sure that the air can move freely and that it can come into contact with all sides. The best way to do this is to hang the cut and cleaned branches or use the drying grids if you are working with single lines or small branches. If you choose to use the grids, keep in mind that you need to turn the ropes upside down regularly to make sure they do not flatten on one side.

For best results, you should hang (or otherwise place the cut ropes in a dark room with good air circulation and a relative humidity of about 45-55%.

Time Needed to Dry Cannabis Properly

There are many factors that influence the time it takes for cannabis to dry.

The size of your buds will obviously affect the drying time, as larger and denser buds will take longer to dry than smaller buds. The way you choose to trimming your plants will also matter. Remember that the branches of your plants contain more water, so if you hang large branches, they will take longer to dry than smaller branches or individual buds. Finally, the temperature, humidity and airflow in your drying space will also have a big impact on the time it takes for the grass to dry.

Generally, the drying phase takes about 7-12 days, depending on the factors mentioned above. During this period, your buds will lose a lot of water, which means they will shrink in size and also lose a lot of weight.

There is a simple test to see if your buds are dry: just take a small branch and try to bend it. If it breaks, your buds are dry and you are ready to go through the tanning process. If it bends, your buds need a little more time to dry.

How can I tune my tops?

If you've trimmed the wet peaks, you'll be ready to move on to tanning as soon as they dry. On the other hand, if you have chosen dry trimming, we recommend that you do it before you go into tanning.

Once your tops are dry and clean, place them in large jars with a wide mouth (glass or jam jars work perfectly). Fill the jars about ¾ full, so there is room for extra air and to reduce the risk of mould spoiling your crop. After filling the jars, store them in a dark, dry place (like the cupboard) and check your tops at least once a day for two weeks.

During this check, keep the jars open to allow for air exchange and inspect each line individually for any signs of mould. If you find an infected line, be sure to remove it immediately from the jar to prevent the fungus from spreading.

This process of constantly checking the ropes will remove excess moisture from the pots and allow the grass to come into contact with fresh air. After about two weeks, you can start enjoying the harvested grass, but the longer you wait, the better.

Most growers will have their grass tanned for about a month, but tanning for 4-8 weeks will get the maximum flavour and aroma from your buds.

How to store the tops after they've been dried and tanned.

Once the tanning is finished, you can store the tops in the same jars, in a cool, dark and dry place. You no longer need to check the tops as often, so make sure you keep the pots tightly closed to prevent the flowers from drying out too much. If you have a lot of grass, consider investing in humidifying packages or something similar to keep your flowers fresh for long periods of time.

CHAPTER 24 – Pests, Mushrooms, Moulds

Marijuana is certainly among the most resistant commercial crops, a plant that grows on all continents. Unfortunately, things can go wrong even in indoor or outdoor crops followed with the greatest care and attention. However, by taking some preventive measures, the chances of obtaining healthy, strong crops without any difficulty increase dramatically.

Indoor growers have a greater degree of control over environmental parameters, but outdoor growers can and should also apply two basic principles to each crop. Firstly, the growing space, which should always be clean and tidy. Secondly, isolate the crops as much as possible. Good cleanliness can do a lot in a cannabis crop. Poor hygiene in a growing area is an open invitation to pathogens. Isolating cannabis plants in a secluded place avoids the unintentional introduction of pathogens.

Of course, cannabis plants will never be able to tell you what problem they have, but they will express some symptoms. It will be up to the grower to accurately diagnose the problem and then apply the appropriate treatment. However, you can only intervene if you know what to look for. Look carefully at your diseased cannabis plants and read the next section to find the right solution.

Grey Mould

Recognize Grey Mould, also known as Botrytis Cinerea or Grey Rot). One way to detect the presence of grey mould in time is to keep an eye on the leaf growing from the inflorescences. When they take on a strange colour (see photos below) and are torn off by the inflorescence with a gentle tear, you can be 99% sure that there is rot in the bud.

SPREAD OF GREY MOULD

The cause of grey mould includes dead leaves falling with the arrival of autumn, spider webs, larvae and insect eggs... everyone can rot in your plant. The most common cause is pythium, a very common fungus in cannabis. This fungus causes the roots to rot and the lower part of the stem to rot. Larger, healthier plants are less sensitive to pythium. In a serious pythium infestation plants fall ill with "tipping sickness", and we don't have to explain to you what that means.

Pythium can be recognized by how the bark turns brown at the base of the stem. At first the brown scales can be easily removed, but later the rotting process becomes deeper and deeper into the base of the plant.

Pythium is a mould, which develops best in wet and humid environments. Pythium brides only spread via water. Two types of spores form: zoospores and passive spores. The zoospores germinate better at a temperature of 15° C, whilst the passive spores begin to grow with heat, therefore at about 28° C.

A constant soil temperature is recommended to prevent pythium infestations. Too wide fluctuations in temperature should be avoided. You also need a good level of humidity (i.e. not too high).

Leaf mould, rust and fungi are less common than pythium. Rust can cause grey mould among other symptoms. Other causes of Grey Mould include autumn fall of leaves, spider webs, larvae and insect eggs.

PREVENT GRAY MOLD

Prevention is difficult in the climates of Western European nations, because this mould prefers low temperatures and high humidity - things that are quite inevitable in this part of the world. Try to keep plants as dry as possible. For example, it is a good idea to shake the morning dew off the plants every day, and to place them in direct sunlight and in a place where the wind provides sufficient ventilation. The optimal situation is to bring the plants indoors every night to avoid the worst cold and humidity. Placing the plants above ground level can also help to keep the temperature more stable by increasing resistance dramatically, allowing them to fight disease.

Another solution for next year is to darken the plants early so that they can bloom before the autumn humidity comes. The inflorescences will then take full advantage of the months of summer sunshine and will be of better quality.

It may also be worth spraying the plants with Bayer's Teldor spray during the growing period, twice (or once Teldor and once Finesse to prevent resistance from developing), and again at the beginning of flowering. During flowering, spray only the stems. Teldor binds with the waxy layer of the leaf and is not washed off easily.

FIGHT GREY MOULD

The only thing you can do against grey mould during flowering is to prune the infected branches and sterilize your scissors between each cut. You are dealing with a fungus and the fungi release spores that can very easily infect other parts of the plant. It is worth trying to cover the infected foliage with plastic bags before cutting them to reduce the spread of spores.

So, work with precision and a lot of hygiene, and constantly check your plants for new infections. As soon as you find a beginning of rotting in the plant, it's a losing battle, so in case of a real emergency the best thing to do is to harvest everything the plant has already produced hoping to save some of the harvest.

In case mould has attacked the stem and branches can be kept reasonably under control by spreading the affected area with old style "green soap", a well-known brand of cleaning paste that is sold in pots, applied with a small brush. The basic (alkaline) environment will stop the mould, the stain will turn black and the deterioration will stop. Just be careful not to rub it on the inflorescences! I have used it for years in case of infection and it has guaranteed a good durability of branches and stems, blocking the spread of spores.

Another option is to remove as much of the infected areas as possible and then rub gently with a 3-10% hydrogen peroxide (hydrogen peroxide) solution. The stems and stem can also be rubbed with a mixture of Teldor, bleach and Dettol (do not drop it on the roots!).

Mould

The Mildew is the generic name given for a number of mould infections that can affect our plants, in which various parts of the plant are covered with white mould or downy grey mould. True mould (Erysiphe graminis) is common on various types, with various specialized forms (forma specialis) each specifically adapted to a variety.

TRUE MOULD

Mildew: The real mould forms a downy mildew on the top surface of the leaf

FAKE MOULD

Fake mould: Fake mould appears on the underside of the leaf. The fake mould is found on, cucumbers, lettuce and other plants

MOLDS, WHICH MAKE OUR PLANTS ROT

Mould tends to thrive in humid conditions, especially if there is not enough air circulating. In these conditions the mould spores, which are always present in the air, find a place where they can establish a foothold and begin to grow into adult fungi. If you have failed to prevent the growth of these fungi, then you need to get to grips with the situation as quickly as possible.

If fungal growth is still moderate, simply remove the infected parts immediately and make sure that the cannabis growing environment is suitable for growing plants rather than mould, i.e. with good ventilation, temperature and humidity control, and that the plants are not in a soil that is too wet.

If the infestation is more serious, there is no choice but to spray poison (fungicide). Repeat the application again after a couple of days, although it may seem that the first application has clarified the problem. Also, in this case, we repeat that you need to control the climate, improving it with the advice given before. The application of the fungicide should be considered as a last resort. It is not healthy for young plants or people, so this is another case where it is always better to prevent than to cure.

Leaf mould (like Mildew) and filamentous fungi are less common than Pythium. Mildew can cause, among other things, rotting of the tops. Here too, the same precautions can help: maintain optimal climate control. Unlike many other moulds, mildew can grow even when the moisture content of the air is low.

The Bud rot usually strikes towards the end of the flowering phase. And the more compact the plant, the more likely it is that this disease can affect the plant. You can recognize the rot bud by the way the leaves on the top suddenly turn yellow. This yellow also leaves the top off the plant by applying a very low force. To prevent the whole plant from contracting the infection, I am afraid that you will have to remove all the buds and branches with this infection.

The Bud rot can be prevented to some extent by ensuring that your growing space has relatively low air humidity, even during dark periods.

COMBAT

It was only about three years ago that researchers in South America approached alternative prevention for mildew. Brazilian scientist Wagner Bettiol discovered that one spray a week with milk could keep mildaew infection under control, as if it were a spray with synthetic pesticides.

Not only was milk a good protection for the plant, it also proved to be a very useful dietary supplement for the leaves, a good way to boost the plant's immune system. The results of his experiments showed that a weekly spray with a concentration of at least 10% (1-part milk to 9 parts water) reduces the extent of mould infestation by 90%. Just be careful not to increase the concentration of the milk too much, as a concentration above 30% starts to serve as a basic nutrient for the leaf infection. That is, above 30% helps the infection.

Tobacco Mosaic Virus (TMV)

The Tobacco Mosaic Virus belongs to the Virgaviridae family which consists of very small rods about 700 nanometres long. On a plant affected by this virus you will see that the youngest leaves will start to produce yellow-green ring spots, circular shapes and serpentine lines. Older leaves, on the other hand, will produce a yellow mosaic. The leaves will turn completely yellow in a short time. Sometimes the virus hits the plant without these symptoms becoming visible.

THE SPREAD OF TMV

An attack by the Tobacco Mosaic Virus appears more in Summer and Autumn, when there are a lot of flying aphids around the plants. Aphids can easily introduce the virus into plants. When you work around your plants you can also inadvertently spread the virus in a lesser way. Spreading through seeds or soil is not possible.

The virus has various carriers, including lettuce and various species of grass, can also survive in these plants. The virus also infects other commercial plants, such as tobacco, watermelon, tomatoes and others. Cross infection is possible (From grass to tomato and vice versa.).

From the moment the virus enters the plant there is no chance of it getting out again; and clones made after the plant infection will also be infected with the TMV virus.

Warning: The Tobacco Mosaic Virus (TMV) can also be found in cigarettes and packaged tobacco!!

EFFECTS IN PLANTS

The effects in the plants are very different, and the plant will never recover the previous strength because due to the state in which the leaves will be, the chlorophyll photosynthesis will remain forever reduced. The plant will never become one of the best plants, this is one of the safe things, and in general it will always be underdeveloped.

FIGHT TMV

As mentioned earlier, there are no real solutions since the virus entered the plant. But environmental factors are important; a plant in a constant ambient temperature of 21 degrees Celsius or even higher temperature will have less problems from the virus, so keeping plants at a temperature of 21 degrees Celsius and above is essential.

PREVENT TMV

The first step is to make sure you start growing your plants in a really clean place, so make sure the place has as few bugs as possible and wash your hands every time before you start "playing" with your plants.

If the virus can reach the big plant, then there is a 99% chance that you will either let it grow in the whole growing space as well. In the beginning there is already a chance of detecting the virus in a clone if there has also been infection in the clone. So, inspect each clone carefully. If you notice that the plant will have strange characteristics, simply forget about it and throw it away and use another one.

In order to drastically reduce the chances of infection you will have to start planting your plants from good and safe clones or you can start making your own clones. You may also decide to start planting from seeds, which will reduce the chances of a TMV infection to a minimum.

The most important question, of course, is how much does it affect your crop? The answer is considerably. Because your plants that have the virus will have ruined the leaves and this will make them produce less. But if you can keep the temperature from 21 degrees Celsius and up, the damage will be much less and you can live with it, but if the TMV virus hits your plants outdoors, they will have a lot of stress to deal with if you live in a place where the ambient temperature is below 21 degrees Celsius.

Yellow spots on the leaf

The yellow spot on the leaf, or "Septoria leaf" is a malignant fungal pathogen that causes lesions on the leaves of cannabis plants. This infection starts with the older leaves on the bottom of the plant. Initially yellow spots appear on the leaves. Later these parts dry out and the spores proliferate. The leaves will turn brown, die and fall off. If not treated, this infection will spread between the leaves and is highly contagious to the rest of the plants in cultivation.

YELLOW SPOTS ON THE LEAF: CAUSES

The humid environmental conditions, where moisture accumulates on the leaves, is the perfect fertile soil for fungi. High levels of relative humidity in cultivation or heavy rainfall on outdoor crops are almost always associated with epidemics. Poor airflow is also a factor that contributes greatly to infections.

YELLOW SPOTS ON THE LEAF: CURES

Unfortunately, there is no cure for leaf Septoria. The affected areas must be removed surgically. Fungal spores can spread very easily. You need to use a pair of latex gloves and prune using sterile scissors. Collect all the removed leaves immediately while cutting the infected material. Be careful not to drop anything into the pots, or onto the ground if you grow outdoors, because the fungus will spread there too.

After the leaves have been removed, take a tour of your local shop. The remaining healthy leaves and stems can be sprayed with a specific copper-based fungicide. But if you are dealing with this problem during flowering, it is not advisable to spray this product.

YELLOW SPOTS ON THE LEAF: COUNTERMEASURES

Indoor growers can avoid this pathogen by monitoring environmental conditions and keeping relative humidity under control. A thermo-hygrometer can give you all the temperature and relative humidity data you need at a glance. Adding a simple oscillating fan or a clip fan in tighter spaces can greatly improve airflow and reduce the humidity on the leaves. Avoid over-watering and even pots exposed to rainwater.

Radical rot

Root rot is a disease that can affect the roots of cannabis plants and is difficult to detect until it is too late. Dropping, rickety plants that appear to lack water or over-watering can actually suffer from root rot. Using some systems, hydro growers can take a look and see if the roots are discoloured, brown or balled up and covered in mud. As for coconut and soil growers, it is very likely that a rotten smell will alert them.

RADICAL ROOTS: CAUSES

Too little oxygen and too much water in the root zone usually leads to putrefaction. Algae, bacteria and fungi can all be responsible for the infection. Sick plants are more sensitive, but even perfectly healthy plants can be infected. Many fungi that can cause root rot can in fact survive in the surface layer of the soil and in plant waste if the cultivation is poorly cared for.

RADICAL ROTTING: CURES

Radical rot can really be a crop killer. The only medicine is to return the grow box or garden to a root-friendly condition as soon as possible. Sterilize and start again. Under no circumstances should you reuse the same growing medium. Specialized products on the market today can be useful, but nothing can cure root rot hoping for a high success rate.

RADICAL ROT: COUNTERMEASURES

Hydroponic growers need to check the water levels in the reservoir and make sure the air pumps are working to maintain the right oxygen supply. It may be necessary to switch to chemically based nutrients if algae are a problem. Soil and coconut growers also need to provide plants with good aeration in the root zone. Always use cannabis-specific substrates that drain well.

Don't be afraid to add more perlite to the substrates to improve drainage. Make sure the plants are not in rainwater puddles and consider using Air-Pot instead of normal plastic pots. Of course, adding beneficial microorganisms to the water and substrates helps to create a stronger and more resistant root zone.

Peronospora (Downy mildew)

Downy mildew is not a cannabis disease but rather a combination of common symptoms associated with a variety of fungal and bacterial infections. Think of weak plants with chlorosis and a stunted and abnormal growth.

DOWNY MILDEW: CAUSES

High humidity, over-watering and poor cleaning can irreparably damage cannabis plants. Ultimately, grower error is often the cause. It is the grower's responsibility to maintain an efficient wet and dry cycle in the root zone and to keep cannabis cultivation clean.

DOWNY MILDEW: CARE

The only cure is to correct the mistake you made. Growers need to continuously monitor environmental conditions and plant behaviour to identify problems. Many growers keep a cultivation diary to keep track of the results and learn something from each cycle.

DOWNY MILDEW: COUNTERMEASURES

Growers who develop a precise nutrition program and daily plant care routine are less likely to encounter downy mildew. The more you can control environmental conditions and nutrients, the better. Healthy cannabis plants grown under very near optimal climatic conditions will not succumb to downy mildew.

Mushroom flies

A clear sign of infestation is the presence of midges buzzing around your precious plants, or crawling on the soil where they live. However, given their minute size, it is easy not to notice them until it is already too late and you start to produce problems. Other signs to take seriously are the pale leaves, darkening leaf contours, and dark spots on the leaves. Other signs include leaves that become soft, twisting and yellowing. Symptoms that manifest themselves throughout the plant may be slower growth of the buds and roots, and general withering.

PREVENT INFESTATIONS

Prevention is better than cure. First and foremost, because following these measures can protect your marijuana plants from infestation, saving you time and money to fight the gnats once they have settled.

One concrete way to make sure these bastards don't start colonizing the soil of your grass plants is to pay close attention to the amount of water you give them, and the frequency with which you water them. Too much water will create the perfect, moist breeding ground for the growth of fungi, and consequently the attacks of midges. It is advisable to always let the first couple of centimetres of the soil surface dry before watering the plants again. In doing so, you will avoid creating an unfavourable environment.

Placing a protective screen on the growing medium, such as a tissue, is a good way of defending against spawning. Other obvious safeguards include keeping windows, nets, and screens as closed as possible.

If you are growing outdoors, you have far less control over the conditions than in an indoor artificial environment. However, there are many ways to prevent gnats from nibbling on your plantation. One option is to sterilise your potting soil to make sure that pestiferous eggs are not lying in wait for you. Some growers go as far as using predatory insects to annihilate those who are plundering your plants. Planting garlic and onions near your plants can also form a defensive shield that will keep predators at bay.

WHAT TO DO WHEN INFESTATIONS OCCUR

Inspect your plants every day. Just as you take the time to appreciate their magnificent appearance and aroma, make a quick check to identify any possible symptoms of gnats. The sooner you realise they are there, the quicker you can remedy them.

If you are unlucky enough to find that an invasion has already occurred, there are several ways to deal with the problem. First of all, place flycatcher sheets of yellow stickers in the growing area; their bright colour attracts the gnats and traps them in the glue on the cards. This will help reduce the total number of gnats attacking your marijuana, and it will also be a useful technique to realise the seriousness of the situation.

Secondly, as mentioned above, analyse your watering methods. Stop watering until the ground surface is dry. This will reduce the amount of fungi in the soil and starve the larvae to death. To speed up the drying process of the soil, aim a light fan at the soil surface.

Applying neem oil to the soil is a good way to counteract the problem; it has proven to be very effective in eliminating fungus gnats and other possible latent plagues. Spreading food-grade kieselguhr (or diatomaceous earth or diatomaceous earth) on the soil may also help, as it is a natural and organic insecticide derived from fossilized shells.

Certain bacteria can be introduced into the soil to destroy invading gnats. However, some of these bacteria can actually damage beneficial microbes in the soil, which will take time to reform. For this reason, it is better to use more delicate methods, such as an organic version of Bacillus thuringiensis.

Aphids

The term aphid is used to refer to a group of sap-sucking parasites that are among the most destructive to plants.

The size of aphids varies approximately 1 to 10 millimetres (0.04 to 0.39 inches). They can be green, black, red or white. The most common type of aphid found in home gardens is usually green, and about 1 millimetre long.

These insects have two whip-like antennae at the end of the head, and a pair of tube-shaped structures facing the back end of the animal's body.

Female winged aphids usually lay their eggs in early spring, and give rise to more female larvae. After a few weeks, these larvae are mature enough to procreate in turn. The process is repeated several times, and the number of aphids can increase considerably in a very short time.

By the end of summer, the aphids develop sexual traits (male and female), and mate to produce eggs for wintering. Most aphids, except for specimens with sexual traits, do not need to mate to reproduce. They are able to reproduce by parthenogenesis.

There are over 4,000 different species of aphids worldwide. Some species of aphids are able to develop wings.

HOW TO DETECT APHIDS ON CANNABIS PLANTS

Aphids can usually be noticed on the leaves and stems of the cannabis plant. Green species can be more difficult to detect. In particular, they tend to hide on the back of the leaves, avoiding direct exposure.

Aphids feed by sucking sap from plants. During this process they release a thick, sticky substance called honeydew, which promotes the development of black, sooty mould. Honeydew also attracts ants, which could protect the aphids from other predatory insects. This can make the infestation even worse.

When they feed, the aphids cause the leaves to curl. They then wither or turn yellow and the development of the plant stops. Aphids are also able to transmit diseases and spread them when they pass on other plants to feed.

HOW TO CONTROL/PREVENT APHIDS ON CANNABIS

A small colony of aphids doesn't usually cause big problems. However, aphids are able to reproduce very quickly. Massive infestations can have serious effects on cannabis health and plant growth capacity.

Aphids are introduced into gardens through winged "colonisers". They quickly lay their eggs on the new plants they intend to colonise. It is always better to prevent a pest infection than to control it when it is already present. However, preventing an aphid attack can be particularly difficult.

Outdoor gardens are generally more at risk of infestation by aphids.

As mentioned above, winged aphid females generally lay their eggs in spring. New generations of male and female aphids lay their eggs for wintering in late summer. If you want to protect your garden against any kind of pest, you should make sure that the growing environment is not "inviting" for pests.

Most plant pests love warm, humid and stagnant air. Therefore, it is essential to ensure that the grow room is kept at the correct temperature (ideally between 20°C and 25°C or 68°F and 77°F). It is also advisable to position some fans to ensure good air recirculation.

In any case, to protect yourself optimally against any parasite, you can try some of the tips below. Always keep your eyes open to detect any aphids during spring and late summer.

CLEAN UP INFECTED AREAS

If you notice aphids on your plants, the first step in treating the infection is to cut off the affected parts and immediately throw them in the trash.

After pruning the plants, you should rinse them with water, or a solution of water and vinegar, to remove any surviving insects.

INTRODUCE PREDATORY INSECTS

Ladybirds, hoverflies, hymenoptera, aphidoletes aphidimyza, tomisids (crab spiders) and chrysopids are natural predators of aphids and other harmful parasites (such as red spiders and whiteflies).

We recommend introducing some of these insects into your garden during spring and late summer to best prevent infestations. If you have already noticed the presence of aphids on plants, it is usually too late at this point to exploit predatory insects.

You can follow some of the other tips below. After eliminating aphids, you can introduce predatory insects back into your garden as a prevention for future attacks.

USE ORGANIC INSECTICIDES

For aphids and any other type of parasite, we recommend avoiding the use of chemical pesticides. They are in fact unsafe for contact with cannabis plants. You can try some of these options:

Essentria IC3: Essentria IC3 combines several oils of vegetable origin. It is a biological insecticide that we recommend to keep always available. It can be applied directly to plants and helps prevent the attack of many pests, including red spiders, whitefly and aphids.

Remember that the product remains active for 8-12 hours. Therefore, it is advisable to apply it every day until the parasites are completely eliminated.

Spinosad: All Spinosad products are totally organic and should always be present in the gardening tools of any cannabis grower. Like Essentria, Spinosad can be sprayed directly on cannabis plants. It is able to kill most pests by contact. After eliminating the pest invasion, you can add Spinosad into the irrigation water to protect the plants from future attacks.

Insecticide soaps: Insecticide soaps are perfect for treating infected areas of plants locally. They can eliminate most pests (such as red spiders and whiteflies). However, it is advisable to avoid applying the product directly to the buds of cannabis. As with Spinosad and Essentia, we recommend applying the insecticide soap at least twice to ensure total elimination of aphids.

TREATMENT WITH OILS

Some growers firmly believe in the effectiveness of vegetable oils and essential oils to control and prevent garden pests such as aphids. Neem oil is very often used to protect plants from pests. There are also many other oils that seem to have the same protective qualities, such as eucalyptus, rosemary, lemon and cinnamon oils.

Just mix these oils in a little water, and spray the solution evenly on the plants with a nebulizer. Most essential oils contain substances that can eliminate parasites on simple contact.

Be careful not to spray the oils on the buds, as you may alter their aromatic profile.

Alternatively, you can regularly apply vegetable oils to your plants. In particular, we recommend canola oil, soya bean oil, or cotton oil.

They give off a faint smell that does not alter the taste and aroma of the cannabis buds.

Ants

To eliminate any insects potentially harmful to our plants, it is always best to avoid chemicals and pesticides. Use organic pesticides, such as **cinnamon** pesticides (easy to make and apply).

Look carefully at the soil or substrate of the pot you are growing. If you are lucky, the ant infestation is only just beginning and only small portions of the soil have been able to colonize. Take a spoonful of cinnamon powder and spread it over the surface of the soil, where you suspect the ants are building their nests. The strong taste of cinnamon should be enough to scare off the ants intent on building colonies.

If the powdered cinnamon does not give the desired results, try to dissolve a couple of teaspoons of cinnamon in distilled water (in the same proportions that you normally use to water plants) and pour the mixture onto the surface of the soil. Let the mixture of cinnamon and water act. This is an infallible remedy for quickly removing ants from your plants.

Neem oil is a valuable ally for all those who grow cannabis organically. This essential oil comes from the neem tree, and contains powerful insecticide substances. It has been used in horticulture, and also in ethnomedicine, for centuries. It can be sprayed directly on plants during the vegetative phase as a pesticide with immediate effect, or once a week or so as a preventive measure against mites, whiteflies, fungus gnats, nematodes and all the other odious creatures that usually attack our plants. Neem oil is not harmful to other beneficial animals such as ladybugs, bees and earthworms, and can also be added to the water with which it is watered to prevent root rot.

A good pesticide mixture can be prepared with 1 teaspoon of neem oil and just 5 drops of surfactant per litre of water. A surfactant, like dish soap, is useful because neem oil does not mix well with water. Using hot water makes the mixing process even easier; just wait for the mixture to cool before applying it to your plants. A nebulizer, set with the finest possible spray, will be needed to wet the surface and the reverse side of all the leaves. All ants sprayed with neem oil will suffer from severe respiratory problems and all others will escape as quickly as they can. Avoid using neem oil directly on the inflorescences of flowering plants.

The use of kieselguhr is a healthy and natural way to prevent pests that do not harm the plants or those who grow them by releasing toxic chemicals. Kieselguhr, also called diatomaceous earth, is a siliceous rock that is derived from the fossil remains of small shelled creatures. It can be easily crumbled into dust, and has many industrial applications. Diatomaceous earth is an excellent mechanical insecticide and this is what arouses the interest of cannabis growers.

The abrasive nature of this 'shell powder' scrapes off the exoskeleton of insects as they pass through, while its high porosity absorbs the vital fluids of all those beasts. Not exactly the environment that the ants will try to colonize, and not even something the pests are able to develop resistance to, unlike chemicals. In addition, diatomite improves the soil's ability to preserve moisture, retaining water and slowing it down, and increasing the oxygenation of the substrate. Caution is required when handling diatomite as it can irritate the skin, eyes and respiratory tract.

Pythium

Pythium is an invisible enemy that attacks the root systems of Cannabis plants, both indoor and outdoor.

This stealthy pathogen is a fungus with a very bad habit of causing chaos in the root portions of plants, especially in hydroponics and overly humid substrates.

A Cannabis plant can be attacked by pythium at any stage of its life cycle. This is why it is essential to avoid over-watering the substrates and creating the most favourable conditions for the development of fungi.

As a root pest, pythium can often go unnoticed by cannabis growers until it has spread throughout the substrate, making possible treatments in vain.

Pythium has the ability to damage the roots of a plant long before the first symptoms appear on the epigeal part of the plants. In fact, the first alarms are usually triggered when the leaves begin to feel its effects.

HOW TO DETECT PYTHIUM

Finding the presence of pythium inside a plantation can be a real puzzle. Outdoor and indoor growers using soil are not immune to root fungal plagues. In fact, its presence is even more difficult to identify in an organic soil than in a hydroponic plant.

However, if you are a hydroponic grower, you should always pay special attention to pythium attacks. However, this type of cultivation has the advantage that you can frequently check the health of the roots.

Of course, hydroponic plants such as Hempy Buckets and organic soil/coco substrates do not allow this advantage.

Colour variations towards brown and small masses in and around the roots can indicate the presence of pythium and therefore root rot. 9 times out of 10 it is this fungus that rots the roots of a plant.

Indoor growers who have had the misfortune to see the consequences of a pythium attack will hardly forget the colour and consistency of the rotting roots.

As well as looking really disgusting, pythium also tends to give off very unpleasant moldlike odours. A plant grown in soil with aesthetic problems apparently related to a root problem is not always the victim of a fungus. Symptoms could result from over-fertilisation, burning from sunshine or lamps or many other factors.

The main signs of apical rot are the leaves that tend to bend downwards, crumpling and detaching from the branches. The possible whitish and brown spots and the yellowish shades of the leaves could easily confuse the grower, leading him to a wrong diagnosis.

HOW TO KEEP THE ROOT ZONES FREE FROM PYTHIUM

By the time you sow a seed, you are already committed to taking care of its initial development stages in order to achieve an optimal Cannabis harvest. Germination is a very important stage on which the final results of a crop depend, which is why we recommend our Royal Queen Seeds Starter Kit. This kit gives you everything you need to follow your plants in their early stages of life and includes a miniature propagator, a germination substrate and of course top-quality feminized seeds.

During the vegetative growth phase, especially when it's time to transplant, plants run the risk of suffering severe shock and/or stress during the change of substrate. Therefore, try to perfectly balance the nutrients, environmental conditions and other parameters that could favour the development of pythium.

This fungus loves Cannabis plants grown in water saturated substrates and if the roots are directly in contact with an inert substrate immersed in water then the conditions will be even more favourable for this micro-predator. Try to fertilise your plants only when they need it and make sure to respect wet-dry cycles when watering so as to limit the moisture content of the substrate.

Those who grow with hydroponic systems must constantly oxygenate the water in the main deposit, not only to ensure optimal nutrient assimilation, but also because pythium tends to die when a substrate is well oxygenated. In such cases, growers using aeroponic systems should not have any such problems!

In hydroponic crops it would be convenient to invest in quality air pumps to keep the water moving and at room temperature. Pythium prefers poorly oxygenated and warm water, where it can spread its spores. Ideally, oxygenation devices should always be placed between the roots and the reservoir, in order to keep the areas close to the root system moving and avoid fungus attacks.

The so-called "air-pots" are pots specially designed to facilitate air circulation between the roots and offer excellent results both in old school soil cultivation and in more advanced and automated hydroponic plants. They cost a few Euros more than normal plastic pots, but tend to have far fewer problems with pythium.

Proper root system development can also be encouraged by adding beneficial bacteria and fungi to the substrate. The grower of the 21st century is fortunate to be able to use a wide range of products containing additives and beneficial substances for the subsoil.

Some products may be far too expensive, but others can be an excellent investment, such as cheap mycorrhiza and/or liquid enzymes, which will pay for themselves at harvest time.

HOW TO TREAT PYTHIUM

We have good news and bad news about possible treatments for pythium. The good news is that pythium can be treated and eliminated, the bad news is that it could involve very high expenses, a high price to pay to defeat an enemy difficult to eradicate.

On the market you can find several products specially formulated to treat radical rot, but their effectiveness is certainly part of the high-end fungicides. Moreover, they are almost always effective only on plants grown indoors and diagnosed with pythium at an early stage.

In case of root rot, the ideal would be to remove all damaged plants and clean up the whole growing area thoroughly, starting from scratch with new substrates and better hygiene strategies. Put your heart at ease and if you are faced with pythium throw everything away and start again with a new crop.

Fighting pythium can be exhausting and even if you manage to win one day, the damage is such that the plants will never recover their original splendour. This means that growth will be stunted and the final yields will be much lower than expected.

As always, when it comes to pests and diseases, prevention is the best medicine and pythium is no exception.

CHAPTER 25 - Growing Cannabis Indoor

In this and the following chapters we try to provide a template of all the steps to follow for indoor and outdoor marijuana cultivation, even if they have already been covered before.

Indoor growing makes it possible to grow marijuana at any time of the year, regardless of weather conditions. Indoor growing has not only made cannabis cultivation more accessible to everyone, but has above all made it possible, at least for the average marijuana user, not to feed organised crime. If you produce your own marijuana you will no longer need drug dealers. Self-sufficiency is your main goal and if you put your mind to it you can easily achieve it.

Of course, in indoor growing with artificial lights it will be the grower's responsibility to create and maintain the environment in which the plants will grow. It will always be him, and no longer Mother Nature, who has to take care of the cannabis and control all the growth parameters. If you want to start an indoor crop at home and smoke your own weed, you will need to be ready to follow your female marijuana plants closely for at least 3 months.

Cannabis growing is a rather concrete activity that requires specific equipment. Lighting kits, fans and activated carbon filters, pots, fertilizers, substrates and Grow Box cabinets are among the first expenses to be incurred. Each cannabis crop requires an initial investment and fixed costs, such as electricity. However, after one or two harvests, you will find that the costs are much lower than you could spend to buy the same amount from a drug dealer.

Choosing the right variety

In recent times, the vast majority of indoor cannabis varieties have been specially adapted for artificial light cultivation. Cannabis varieties grown outdoors can also be grown indoors. However, outdoor varieties show that they are less flexible when adapting and generally behave better in the open air when the sunlight is strong and warm.

We recommend micro growers and those who use cabinets with limited heights to stick with Indica dominated feminized and/or auto flowering photoperiodic hybrids. Small, bushy plants that complete their life cycle in a short time are also recommended for beginner growers.

Growers who use Grow Boxes or turn entire rooms into cannabis plantations have more options when selecting varieties. Stompier Indica or auto flowering varieties can produce more abundant yields when subjected to the SOG, or Sea of Green, technique.

Alternatively, if you have more than 2 metres of vertical space at your disposal, you could also grow taller, sativa-dominant varieties. Later flowering sativa can stretch significantly during the flowering period. They often require pruning or bending to be controlled during growth.

The variety best suited to the specific conditions of your Grow Room will also be the best plant to grow. Experienced growers use pruning and bending techniques such as LST, Fimming, Topping and ScrOG to make it easier to grow Haze varieties from 13 weeks in flowering. However, unless you already know the variety you are going to grow, you will need to collect as much data as possible from multiple sources to determine if it is more or less suitable for your growing conditions.

Seeds or Clones

Probably the most important thing is to start growing your own grass and continue in this direction. Starting from seed doesn't necessarily take longer. Autoflowering seeds beat photoperiodic clones nine times out of ten in terms of harvest expectations. In addition, using feminized seeds you won't even have to eradicate male plants and you won't inherit any unwanted pests or pathogens often found in other growers' clones. In addition, new and exciting new cannabis strains are constantly being created and you could always arrange with a Cannabis Club in your town to develop cuttings from extraordinary Cannabis Cup winners to meet demand.

Preparation of the cultivation space

A growing environment complete with all the necessary accessories for plant growth can be purchased online in a single package. Normally, these growing kits are divided into three main types of cultivation: organic soil, coconut and hydroponics. The most common remains the Grow Box. Growing marijuana plants inside a

Grow Box located in a guest bedroom has become the standard operating procedure of almost all home growers.

The most modern Grow Boxes are available in different shapes and sizes. Alternatively, you can convert a wardrobe or an entire room. If you opt for DIY gardening, know that not all spaces are suitable for growing. An indoor plantation must be quarantined and requires special reflective sheeting. In addition, the area must be light-tight to avoid interrupting the dark period. You can still try to adapt a corner of the house for your crops.

There are several techniques for growing marijuana indoors. Regardless of the type of marijuana or the particular style you will adopt, every indoor grower needs to control some important factors to grow cannabis correctly: light, water, nutrients, substrate and environmental parameters (temperature, relative humidity and airflow).

Obviously, you will need to constantly monitor these factors in order to manage them correctly. Therefore, you will need one of the most important tools: the thermo-hygrometer. In Grow Rooms it is essential and it is the only means with which you will be able to check variations in temperature and relative humidity. You'll also need a kit or a pen device to control pH, unless you use nutrients that automatically adjust themselves to optimal pH levels.

The lifecycle of cannabis

Indoor growers can decide when to force the flowering of their photoperiodic plants simply by controlling the light cycle of the lamps. If things go wrong, vegetative growth can be extended by maintaining a cycle of 18-6 so that corrections can be made and the plants can recover. Otherwise you might adopt some pruning and bending techniques. In both cases, the vegetative growth time will not necessarily be within the typical 3-6 weeks.

Also, vegetative growth can be reduced by a few weeks, which is particularly useful for sativa growers, switching to the 12-12 light cycle after just 1-2 weeks of vegetative growth. In addition, growers of automatic varieties can help the plants achieve their best performance and speed by experimenting with light cycles of 18-6, 20-4, 22-2 or even 24 hours.

Flowering can be very short, such as 5 weeks for accelerated flowering autoflowering, although the transition always starts about 30 days after germination (regardless of the light cycle provided). Indica varieties finish flowering after about 8 weeks, while Indica-sativa hybrids can take 8-12 weeks. However, there are extraordinary sativa-dominant varieties, such as Amnesia Haze, which can go beyond 12 weeks of flowering.

A layer of resin crystals and white pistils turning to red/orange will alert you that harvest time is approaching. Confirmation will come from the trichomes, which will need to be carefully analysed with a pocket microscope. When their resin heads will be milky white, with other sporadic amber heads, then you can start harvesting.

CHAPTER 26 - Outdoor Cannabis Growing

Growing cannabis outdoors has many advantages. Besides being a very pleasant experience, it allows you to grow larger plants with better yields.

Indoor vs Outdoor

Normally, outdoor growing offers more space to work, plenty of sunshine, free rainwater, better ventilation and the joy of growing weather defying the weather.

However, growing outdoors also presents a number of challenges. Plants are more vulnerable to pests, larger predators, heat waves and frosts.

Indoor growing offers more protection for plants and growers have complete control over their growing environment. They can change temperature and humidity settings and plants can be hidden more easily.

That said, indoor growers usually have less space at their disposal, less chance of achieving high yields and have to bear the cost of electricity bills to run their installations.

Growing cannabis outdoors

ADVANTAGES

- ✓ Larger plants
- ✓ More space
- ✓ Free rainwater
- ✓ Sunlight (cheaper than artificial lighting)
- ✓ No need to change the light cycle
- ✓ Ventilation helps keep mould at bay.
- ✓ Plant association
- ✓ Beneficial insects
- ✓ Soil rich in native microorganisms
- ✓ Opportunities to practice breeding methods

CHOOSE THE AREA

Once you have decided to grow the plants outdoors, you must choose the area in which to grow them. Look for an area where temperatures are stable, with adequate exposure to sunlight and shelter from the weather.

- Temperatures should never drop below 12°C.
- Temperatures must never exceed 30°C
- 6-8 hours of direct sunlight every day (ideal would be a southern exposure)

- Repairing plants from torrential rain and heat waves (under temporary tarpaulins or greenhouses)

After locating the area, choose a variety to grow. You will need to evaluate your growing environment and the types of affects you want to achieve from your cannabis.

If you live in the northernmost regions with short growing seasons, the best choice is resistant and accelerated flowering genetics, such as autoflowering. If you live further south, the towering sativa that take longer to flower can be a great alternative, but hybrids also grow very well under these conditions.

Are you looking for some particular flavour? Check out the terpenic profile of the varieties you are considering. This will give you a more precise overview of the sensory experience. Do you prefer fruity or earthy aromas? Citrus or candy?

You can also use the data released by the seedbank to estimate the size, flowering time and yield of a particular variety. If you can grow freely, consider a high and very productive variety. If you need to grow more discreetly, choose a smaller, stealthy variety.

Germination

The first stage of a cannabis plant's life is germination. During this process, the first taproot root comes out of the seed and will develop into a young seedling. Germination requires three specific factors: darkness, moisture and water. Together, these elements will activate your seeds, and the soil happens to be the ideal place.

Growers living in warm climates can start growing their plants directly in pots or in the open field. However, plants require high humidity during the seedling stage. Consider starting the growth of plants outdoors in a normal greenhouse or in a polyethylene tunnel.

Growers living in cold climates should instead start growing young seedlings in an indoor crop during the colder spring months. Once the climate has warmed up, then the plants can be transplanted directly into the soil or into larger pots in the open air.

Before germinating the seeds, make sure that the soil is of excellent quality. Organic soil provides everything your plants need to thrive: nutrients, beneficial bacteria and synergistic fungi.

To germinate the seeds, make a hole in the soil in your garden or pot. Place the seed in the hole and gently cover it with a little soil. Add water and after 2-7 days your first seedling should sprout.

The seedling stage will last about two weeks. Give the young seedlings adequate lighting, humidity levels of about 70% and water in moderation.

The vegetative phase begins when the seedling stage ends. During this period, your plants will focus on photosynthesis and energy creation to fuel their development. During this phase, numerous larger fan leaves will begin to form. To keep your plants in full shape, follow these tips:

Water only when the first 3-5cm of soil has become dry. If you water too frequently, your plants will become vulnerable to root rot and other problems.

From time to time, test your soil to ensure that it remains within a pH range of 6.0 to 7.0 (the optimum range for nutrient uptake).

Prevent pests

One of the hardest-fought challenges among outdoor growers are pests. Learn how to manage them and prevent their attacks by adopting the following tips.

- Predatory insects: To protect your plants from pests, insert predatory insects into your crops, such as ladybugs and wasps.
- Plant association: Plant basil, lemon balm or dill to repel pests.
- Beneficial mushrooms: Mycorrhizal fungi in the soil can help catch and kill nematodes, soil microorganisms that attack cannabis roots.
- Physical barriers: Install fences made with chicken net and other barriers to prevent larger animals, such as deer and birds, from eating the plants.

Plantula Stadium

The plantula stage lasts about two weeks and precedes the beginning of the vegetative phase. In colder regions it is advisable to continue growing the plants indoors until mid-April. In this way, you will be sure to meet all their temperature and light requirements.

SOWING AND TRANSPLANTING OUTDOORS

If you live in a warmer climate zone, now is the time to germinate the seeds directly outdoors. Now the seedlings grown indoors can be transferred outside and transplanted directly into soil or larger pots.

If you decide to orient your crops according to the lunar cycles, try transplanting when the waning moon enters its ascending phase.

After transplanting, the plants will settle in the soil, continue to grow in the vegetative phase and develop more mass. The transition to summer will give them plenty of light and will continue to stretch upwards, while the North Pole will reach its maximum inclination towards the sun.

Once your plants have settled down, you will be able to plant them and fold them. This will increase yields, open their foliage and make them easier to tame.

Some techniques, such as Low Stress Training, can be adopted between June and July, until the beginning of August. After that, the plants will enter the flowering phase and it will no longer make sense to continue training them.

Prior to flower training, the plants will enter the pre-flowering phase. Use this time interval to check the sex of the plants and prevent any unwanted males from pollinating the female plants. Pre-flowering is formed in the nodes, located where each branch meets the main stem. Remove all males if you do not intend to produce seeds.

The plants have now entered the flowering phase. As the autumn equinox approaches, the days begin to shorten and the plants receive the signal that it is time to flower. Tidy up their branches a bit and make sure that all the sites from which the buds will grow are well exposed to light.

Strip the plants between mid-July and the end of August in preparation for the harvest period. Remove all excess leaves during the waning moon in the decreasing phase.

Perhaps the most exciting time of the entire growth cycle occurs between mid-September and mid-November. The fun part of your hard work has arrived and you can finally harvest your precious inflorescences. The weather is getting cooler, the days are getting shorter and the winter solstice is approaching.

CONCLUSION

Thank you for coming all the way to the end of this book, we hope it was informative and able to provide you with all the tools you need to achieve your goals, whatever they may be.

Growing marijuana for personal use is a great way to get a genuine and tasty product.

Yet, many people fail to get all the benefits of this wonderful process due to lack of knowledge of the process. This book has tried to bring all the important points to the fore so that you can get all the benefits of both indoor and outdoor cultivation without having to deal with the negative effects.

All you have to do is follow the information provided in the book and follow the directions.

You can also get all the benefits of the process by following the simple steps in the book.

I hope this book will really help you achieve your goals.

9 781804 319185